POULTRY AND GAME

Edited by Norma MacMillan and Wendy James
Home economist Gilly Cubitt

ORBIS PUBLISHING London

Introduction

Poultry and game have always been firm favourites for family meals. You'll find lots of new ways of preparing them in this book.

Both imperial and metric measures are given for each recipe; you should follow only one set of measures as they are not direct conversions. All spoon measures are level unless otherwise stated. Pastry quantities are based on the amount of flour used. Dried herbs may be substituted for fresh herbs; use one-third of the quantity.

Photographs were supplied by Editions Atlas, Editions Atlas/Masson, Editions Atlas/Zadora, Barry Bullough, Melvin Grey, Archivio IGDA, Dave Jordan, Lavinia Press Agency, Orbis GmbH, Roger Phillips

The material in this book has previously appeared in *The Complete Cook*

First published 1984 in Great Britain by Orbis Publishing Limited, 20-22 Bedfordbury, London WC2

ISBN 0-85613-578-X
Printed in Italy

Contents

Chicken and clam chowder

Overall timing 1 hour

Freezing Not suitable

To serve 6–8

2lb	Potatoes	900g
	Salt and pepper	
8	Chicken pieces	8
4oz	Butter	125g
15oz	Can of condensed cream of mushroom soup	425g
8oz	Peas	225g
7oz	Can of clams	200g
4 tbsp	Chopped parsley	4x15ml

Peel and dice the potatoes. Cook in boiling salted water for 8 minutes.

Meanwhile, bone the chicken and cut the meat into chunks. Melt the butter in a flameproof casserole, add the chicken and brown lightly.

Tip the soup into a mixing bowl and dilute according to the directions on the can. Add the soup to the chicken, cover and simmer for about 20 minutes.

Drain the potatoes. Add to the casserole and cook for a further 5–7 minutes or till potatoes are just tender. Add peas and cook for 5 minutes longer.

Add the clams with their juice and heat through for 2 minutes. Add a little water, if necessary, and season to taste with pepper.

Stir in the parsley and serve hot.

Cock-a-leekie

Overall timing $2\frac{1}{4}$ hours

Freezing Suitable

To serve 6

2lb	Leeks	900g
1oz	Butter	25g
3lb	Ovenready chicken	1.4kg
3 pints	Stock or water	1.7 litres
1	Bouquet garni	1
	Salt and pepper	
4oz	Prunes (optional)	125g

Wash, trim and slice leeks. Melt butter in a frying pan, add leeks and fry quickly for 5 minutes. Put into a saucepan with the chicken, giblets, stock (made with cubes if necessary) or water, bouquet garni, salt and pepper. Bring to the boil, cover and simmer for $1\frac{1}{2}$ hours.

Stone prunes and add to pan, if using. Cook for 30 minutes longer. Discard bouquet garni.

Remove chicken from pan. Cut the meat into strips, discarding skin and bones. Return meat to pan. Taste and adjust seasoning. Serve with baps or oatcakes.

Chicken and corn soup

Overall timing $1\frac{1}{2}$ hours

Freezing Not suitable

To serve 6

1	Large onion	1
1 oz	Butter	25 g
2 lb	Chicken pieces	900 g
$\frac{1}{4}$ teasp	Ground cumin	1.25 ml
$2\frac{1}{2}$ pints	Chicken stock	1.5 litres
1 lb	Floury potatoes	450 g
	Salt and pepper	
2	Cobs of sweetcorn	2
1	Ripe avocado	1
$\frac{1}{4}$ pint	Plain yogurt or single cream	150 ml

Peel and chop onion. Heat butter in a large saucepan, add chicken and onion and fry for 5 minutes, turning chicken occasionally. Add cumin and fry for 2 minutes. Add stock and bring to the boil. Cover and simmer for 35 minutes till chicken is tender. Meanwhile, peel and dice potatoes.

Lift chicken out of pan. Add potatoes to stock, season and simmer for 10 minutes till tender. Meanwhile, remove skin and bones from chicken and cut flesh into strips. Wash corn, discarding husks. Cut across into 1 inch (2.5 cm) thick slices.

Mash potatoes in the soup to thicken it. Bring to the boil and add corn slices and chicken flesh. Simmer for 10 minutes.

Peel and halve avocado. Remove stone, and slice flesh thinly. Place in a tureen with yogurt or cream. Taste soup and adjust seasoning. Pour into tureen and serve.

Normandy chicken soup

Overall timing 50 minutes

Freezing Suitable: add egg yolk and cream after reheating

To serve 6

8 oz	Chicken breast	225 g
1	Bay leaf	1
$1\frac{3}{4}$ pints	Milk	1 litre
6 tbsp	Calvados or brandy	6x15 ml
8 oz	Button mushrooms	225 g
2 oz	Butter	50 g
4 tbsp	Plain flour	4x15 ml
1 tbsp	Lemon juice	15 ml
$\frac{1}{4}$ teasp	Grated nutmeg	1.25 ml
1 tbsp	Chopped parsley	15 ml
	Salt and pepper	
1	Egg yolk	1
4 tbsp	Single cream	4x15 ml

Put chicken breast in a saucepan with bay leaf and milk and bring to the boil. Cover and simmer for about 15 minutes till tender. Remove chicken from milk. Discard any bones and skin and cut meat into strips. Put into a shallow bowl and pour Calvados or brandy over. Marinate for 20 minutes.

Meanwhile, thickly slice mushrooms. Melt butter in a large saucepan, add mushrooms and fry gently for 5 minutes without browning. Stir in flour and cook for 1 minute. Gradually add strained milk and bring to the boil, stirring. Add lemon juice and nutmeg and simmer for 5 minutes.

Add chicken and marinade with parsley and seasoning. Simmer for a further 5 minutes.

Lightly beat egg yolk and cream in a bowl. Pour in a little of the soup, stirring constantly. Pour back into the soup and cook, stirring, for 3 minutes; do not boil. Serve hot.

Mulligatawny soup

Overall timing $2\frac{1}{2}$ hours

Freezing Not suitable

To serve 6

1	Carrot	1
1	Leek	1
1	Bouquet garni	1
1	Strip of lemon rind	1
$2\frac{1}{2}$ lb	Boiling chicken	1.1 kg
3 pints	Water	1.7 litres
1	Large onion	1
1 oz	Butter	25 g
1 tbsp	Mild curry powder	15 ml
1 teasp	Ground turmeric	5 ml
3 tbsp	Plain flour	3x15 ml
3 oz	Long grain rice	75 g
	Salt	
4 tbsp	Plain yogurt	4x15 ml

Peel and chop the carrot. Trim and chop the leek. Place in a large saucepan with bouquet garni and lemon rind. Add the chicken with the water. Bring to the boil, skim off any scum, cover and simmer for $1\frac{1}{2}$ hours.

Peel and chop the onion. Melt the butter in a flameproof casserole, add onion and fry gently till transparent. Mix the curry powder, turmeric and flour in a small bowl and gradually add $\frac{1}{4}$ pint (150 ml) cold water. Pour into the casserole and bring to the boil, stirring constantly. Remove from heat.

Lift the chicken out of the stock. Strain the stock into the curry sauce a little at a time. Bring to the boil, stirring. Stir in the rice and salt, cover and simmer for 15 minutes.

Meanwhile, cut the chicken into neat pieces, discarding the skin and bones. Add to the soup and simmer for a further 3–5 minutes till the rice is tender. Taste and adjust the seasoning. Put the yogurt into a tureen, pour the soup on to it and serve immediately.

Turkey vegetable soup

Overall timing $1\frac{1}{4}$ hours

Freezing Not suitable

To serve 6

1	Large carrot	1
1	Large onion	1
1	Celery stalk	1
2	Turkey wings	2
$2\frac{1}{2}$ pints	Water	1.5 litres
	Salt and pepper	
8oz	Waxy potatoes	225g
2	Leeks	2
4	Thick slices of bread	4
3oz	Butter	75g

Peel and chop carrot and onion. Trim and chop the celery. Wipe the turkey wings and put into a saucepan with the prepared vegetables, water and seasoning. Bring to the boil, skim off any scum, cover and simmer for 45 minutes.

Peel potatoes and cut into $\frac{1}{2}$ inch (12.5mm) cubes. Trim and slice leeks.

Lift turkey wings out of pan with a draining spoon and leave to cool slightly. Add potatoes and leeks to the soup and simmer for 5 minutes till vegetables are tender.

Remove the skin and bones from the turkey wings and cut the flesh into strips. Add to the soup and reheat gently.

Meanwhile, remove the crusts from bread and cut into cubes. Melt butter in a frying pan, add the bread and fry till golden all over. Drain croûtons on kitchen paper.

Taste soup and adjust seasoning. Pour into a warmed tureen and sprinkle with croûtons. Serve immediately.

Chicken liver soup

Overall timing 20 minutes

Freezing Suitable

To serve 6

1 lb	Chicken livers	450 g
$2\frac{1}{2}$ pints	Chicken stock	1.5 litres
8 oz	Long grain rice	225 g
2 tbsp	Chopped fresh coriander	2x15 ml
1 teasp	Chopped fresh sage	5 ml
	Salt	
	Grated Parmesan cheese	

Wash chicken livers and dice finely.

Bring stock (made with 3 stock cubes if necessary) to the boil in a large saucepan. Add rice and cook for 12–15 minutes or until just tender.

Add livers, coriander and sage. Simmer for a further 2 minutes to cook the livers – they should still be slightly pink inside. Do not over-cook or the livers will toughen and brown and the delicate aroma of the herbs will be lost. Taste and add salt if necessary.

Serve in warmed bowls with grated Parmesan in a separate dish.

Chicken noodle soup

Overall timing 10 minutes

Freezing Not suitable

To serve 4

$2\frac{1}{2}$ pints	Chicken stock	1.5 litres
3 oz	Fine egg noodles	75 g
2 tbsp	Lemon juice	2x15 ml
	Salt and pepper	
2 tbsp	Chopped parsley	2x15 ml

Put the stock into a large saucepan. Bring to the boil and add the noodles. Boil for 3–4 minutes till tender.

Add the lemon juice and seasoning and sprinkle with chopped parsley. Serve with a side dish of grated mature Cheddar cheese.

Chicken liver appetisers

Overall timing 30 minutes

Freezing Suitable (uncooked pastry cases)

Makes 6–8

8 oz	Frozen puff pastry	225 g
1	Egg	1
12 oz	Chicken livers	350 g
1½ oz	Butter	40 g
2-3 tbsp	Marsala	2-3x15 ml
	Salt and pepper	
4 fl oz	Double cream	120 ml

Thaw the pastry, then roll out to about ¼ inch (6 mm) thick. Cut into 2½ inch (6 cm) rounds and place in a dampened baking tray. Cut halfway through the centre of each round with a 1½ inch (4 cm) cutter.

Brush with beaten egg and bake in a preheated 425°F (220°C) Gas 7 oven for 15 minutes or until well risen and crisp.

Meanwhile, finely chop the chicken livers. Cook in the butter until lightly browned. Stir in the Marsala, seasoning and cream, and heat through.

Remove the pastry lids and scoop out any soft pastry from the centres of the cases. Fill with the liver mixture and replace the lids. Serve hot.

Terrine with port

Overall timing 1½ hours plus 12 hours marination

Freezing Suitable

To serve 6

4 fl oz	Port	120 ml
1 teasp	Dried thyme	5 ml
2	Bay leaves	2
½ teasp	Grated nutmeg	2.5 ml
	Salt and pepper	
1 tbsp	Oil	15 ml
12 oz	Chicken livers	350 g
4 oz	Belly of pork	125 g
4 oz	Pie veal	125 g
7 oz	Streaky bacon	200 g

Mix port, thyme, one bay leaf, nutmeg, pepper and oil. Add chicken livers, and marinate in refrigerator overnight.

The next day, mince pork and veal. Remove livers from marinade; chop four and mince rest. Mix minced meats, strained marinade and salt.

Preheat the oven to 350°F (180°C) Gas 4.

Line terrine with two-thirds of bacon. Spread half mince in dish. Cover with chopped livers and top with remaining mince. Press down well. Place remaining bay leaf on top. Cover with rest of bacon, then with foil.

Put dish in tin containing hot water. Cook in oven for about 1 hour. Cool, then turn out for serving.

Game pâté

Overall timing 2 hours plus marination

Freezing Suitable

To serve 6–8

1½ lb	Boned game (venison, hare, grouse, partridge)	700 g
8 oz	Pig's liver	225 g
6	Juniper berries	6
4 tbsp	Gin	4x15 ml
4 oz	Smoked streaky bacon	125 g
8 oz	Fatty bacon	225 g
2	Onions	2
	Salt and pepper	
2 oz	Fresh white breadcrumbs	50 g
½ teasp	Dried marjoram	2.5 ml
8 oz	Pork flare or fatty streaky bacon	225 g

Cut game and liver into small pieces and place in shallow dish. Add crushed juniper berries and sprinkle with gin. Leave to marinate in fridge for at least 2 hours, turning meat occasionally.

Cut streaky and fatty bacon into small pieces. Place in saucepan and cook over low heat until fat runs. Peel and chop onions, add to the pan and cook till transparent.

Drain meat, reserving marinade, and add to saucepan. Season to taste. Cover and simmer for 15 minutes. Remove from heat and leave to cool. Mince mixture coarsely.

Preheat oven to 400°F (200°C) Gas 6.

Add breadcrumbs to the marinade, then minced meats and mix well. Adjust seasoning and add marjoram. Line terrine or dish with two-thirds of pork flare or streaky bacon. Fill with pâté mixture and press down well. Cover with remaining flare or bacon, then with foil, before putting on lid. Place in a roasting tin containing 1 inch (2.5 cm) water. Bake for 1½ hours. Weight and cool.

Piquant liver canapés

Overall timing 45 minutes

Freezing Not suitable

To serve 4

8 oz	Chicken livers	225 g
4 oz	Mushrooms	125 g
1	Onion	1
2 oz	Bacon rashers	50 g
3 oz	Butter	75 g
¼ pint	Chicken stock	150 ml
2 teasp	Tomato purée	2x5 ml
½ teasp	Worcestershire sauce	2.5 ml
	Salt and pepper	
2 tbsp	Chopped parsley	2x15 ml
1 teasp	Lemon juice	5 ml
8	Slices of bread	8
1 tbsp	Grated Parmesan cheese	15 ml

Wipe and trim the livers. Wipe and chop the mushrooms. Peel and finely chop the onion. Derind and chop the bacon.

Heat 1 oz (25 g) of the butter in a pan, add onions and bacon and fry for 5 minutes. Add the liver, mushrooms, stock, tomato purée, Worcestershire sauce and seasoning. Cook for a further 15 minutes, stirring frequently. Remove from the heat and allow to cool slightly.

Purée in a blender or food processor. Return to pan and season to taste. Add parsley and lemon juice. Cook over high heat for 1–2 minutes, stirring constantly to give a thick, spreading consistency.

Toast the bread and cut off crusts, if liked. Spread with remaining butter, cut into quarters diagonally and spread thinly with the liver mixture. Sprinkle with Parmesan. Garnish with parsley. Serve hot.

Chinese chicken parcels

Overall timing $1\frac{1}{2}$ hours

Freezing Not suitable

To serve 4

9 oz	Boned chicken breasts	250 g
2 tbsp	Soy sauce	2x15 ml
1 tbsp	Dry sherry	15 ml
3–4	Spring onions	3–4
	Vegetable oil	
30	Thin slices root ginger	30
8 oz	Cooked green beans	225 g

Cut chicken breasts into very thin, $\frac{1}{2}$ inch (12.5 mm) wide and 1 inch (2.5 cm) long strips. Place in a bowl with soy sauce and sherry. Trim spring onions and shred finely.

Cut bakewell paper into thirty 4 inch (10 cm) squares and brush with vegetable oil. Place a square with one corner pointing to you. Fold point to centre of square. Under this flap, place a few pieces of drained chicken, one piece of spring onion, one slice root ginger and one or two green beans. Fold right hand corner to centre, then left hand corner so points meet. Fold "envelope" in half to make a rectangle, then fold remaining flap to centre.

Heat vegetable oil, about $1\frac{1}{2}$ inches (4 cm) deep, in deep-fryer. Carefully lower six parcels at a time into hot oil and fry for $1\frac{1}{2}$ minutes on each side, turning carefully. Drain parcels on kitchen paper and serve hot.

Vine leaves stuffed with turkey

Overall timing 1 hour 20 minutes

Freezing Suitable

To serve 4

20	Fresh or canned vine leaves	20
1	Onion	1
2oz	Butter	50g
4	Streaky bacon rashers	4
2oz	Long-grain rice	50g
1 pint	Chicken stock	600ml
$\frac{1}{2}$ teasp	Dried thyme	2.5ml
	Salt and pepper	
8oz	Cooked turkey meat	225g
4 tbsp	Chopped parsley	4x15ml

Prepare fresh vine leaves according to the instructions on the packet. Drain canned leaves.

Preheat oven to 350°F (180°C) Gas 4.

Peel and finely chop onion. Heat butter in a frying pan and cook onion till soft. Derind and dice bacon, add to pan and fry for 2–3 minutes.

Add rice and stir until well coated and beginning to turn transparent. Add half the stock, the thyme and seasoning. Cover and cook until stock has been absorbed. Remove from the heat and cool slightly.

Mince turkey very finely and put it in a bowl. Add rice mixture. Season well and stir in parsley.

Divide turkey mixture among vine leaves and roll into tight parcels. Pack into an ovenproof dish and pour over remaining stock. Bake, covered, for 1 hour. Serve hot or cold.

Chicken with blue cheese sauce

Overall timing 30 minutes

Freezing Not suitable

To serve 4

3oz	Butter	75g
4	Boneless chicken breasts	4
¼ pint	Single cream	150ml
5oz	Gorgonzola or other blue cheese	150g
	Pepper	
4 tbsp	Chopped spring onions	4x15ml
2 tbsp	Chopped parsley	2x15ml

Heat 2oz (50g) butter in a frying pan. Add the chicken breasts and fry lightly for about 8 minutes on each side till just tender.

Meanwhile, melt remaining butter in a saucepan. Add cream and bring to the boil, then lower the heat.

Remove any rind from cheese and crumble it into the saucepan. Season well with pepper and add the spring onions. Stir till cheese has melted and sauce is well mixed.

Put chicken breasts on a warmed serving dish and spoon sauce over. Sprinkle with parsley and serve hot.

Grilled chicken breasts with orange basil butter

Overall timing 1 hour

Freezing Suitable

To serve 6

4oz	Butter	125g
2	Oranges	2
	Salt and pepper	
	Cayenne	
4 tbsp	Chopped fresh basil	4x15ml
6	Boneless chicken breasts	6
6 tbsp	Olive oil	6x15ml
$\frac{1}{2}$ teasp	Dried thyme	2.5ml
	Sprigs of basil	

In a small bowl, mash the butter till creamy and smooth. Grate rind of one orange and add to butter. Add salt and cayenne to taste. Cream basil into butter and roll into a sausage shape. Wrap in foil or cling film and freeze for 30 minutes.

Prick chicken breasts with a skewer and lay them in a shallow dish. Sprinkle with oil, thyme, pepper and juice of one orange. Leave to marinate for 30 minutes, turning occasionally.

Preheat the grill.

Put chicken breasts on grill pan. Spoon marinade over and grill for 20 minutes, turning and basting often.

Cut second orange into 6 slices and cut frozen butter into 6 pieces.

Put cooked chicken breasts on a warmed serving dish and garnish each with a slice of orange, a pat of butter and sprigs of basil. Serve hot.

Chicken breasts with wine and almonds

Overall timing 30 minutes

Freezing Suitable

To serve 4

4	Boneless chicken breasts	4
	Salt and pepper	
3 tbsp	Plain flour	3x15 ml
4 oz	Butter	125 g
2 tbsp	Lemon juice	2x15 ml
1	Small onion	1
1	Garlic clove	1
3 oz	Flaked almonds	75 g
4 tbsp	White wine	4x15 ml

Blanch chicken breasts for 2 minutes in boiling salted water. Drain and pat dry on kitchen paper.

Season flour and coat chicken breasts. Heat 2 oz (50 g) butter in a frying pan and gently fry chicken breasts for about 8 minutes till brown on both sides. Add lemon juice and more seasoning. Cover pan and continue to cook gently for 10 minutes till chicken is tender. Transfer chicken to a warmed serving dish.

Peel and finely chop onion and garlic. Heat 1 oz (25 g) butter in the frying pan and sauté almonds, onion and garlic till almonds are golden brown. Add wine and remaining butter, stirring well.

Reheat chicken in the pan if necessary. Serve with almonds and sauce spooned over.

Chicken breasts in crisp cheese coating

Overall timing 25 minutes

Freezing Suitable

To serve 4

2 oz	Plain flour	50 g
½ teasp	Grated nutmeg	2.5 ml
	Salt and pepper	
4	Boneless chicken breasts	4
2	Eggs	2
2 oz	Dried breadcrumbs	50 g
1 oz	Grated cheese	25 g
3 oz	Butter	75 g
4	Lemon wedges	4

Season flour with nutmeg, salt and pepper and use to coat chicken breasts.

Beat eggs with a little salt in a shallow dish. Mix breadcrumbs and cheese in another shallow dish. Dip floured chicken breasts first in egg and then in breadcrumbs mixture, pressing on well.

Heat butter in a large frying pan and fry chicken breasts over a moderate heat for about 15 minutes, turning once, till golden. Serve with lemon wedges.

Savoury stuffed chicken breasts

Overall timing 1 hour

Freezing Suitable

To serve 6

6	Boneless chicken breasts	6
1	Small onion	1
5 oz	Butter	150g
3 oz	Rice	75g
12 fl oz	Chicken stock	350 ml
	Salt and pepper	
1 oz	Raisins	25g
1 oz	Chopped nuts	25g
½	Green apple	½
1 oz	Cheddar cheese	25g
1	Chicken liver	1
½ teasp	Dried thyme	2.5 ml
½ teasp	Brown sugar	2.5 ml
1 tbsp	Chopped parsley	15 ml

Remove skin from chicken breasts and gently pound till thin, taking care not to make any holes. Set aside.

Peel and finely chop onion. Heat 1 oz (25 g) butter in a frying pan and cook onion till soft. Add rice and stir to coat with butter. Cook till rice is turning transparent, then add 3 fl oz (75 ml) stock. Stir well and season. Add raisins and nuts. Cover and simmer for about 10 minutes till rice has absorbed liquid.

Peel, core and dice apple. Finely dice cheese. Add apple and cheese to rice mixture and remove from the heat.

Chop chicken liver and add to rice mixture with thyme and sugar. Mix well.

Divide mixture among chicken breasts and wrap chicken round. Tie rolls with string. Melt 2 oz (50 g) butter in frying pan and brown rolled chicken breasts on all sides. Add remaining stock, cover and simmer for about 25 minutes till chicken is tender.

Transfer chicken breasts to a warmed serving dish. Discard string. Bring pan juices to the boil and whisk in remaining butter. Pour sauce over chicken and sprinkle with parsley.

Chicken Parmesan

Overall timing 30 minutes

Freezing Suitable

To serve 4

4	Boneless chicken breasts	4
	Salt	
2oz	Butter	50g
$\frac{1}{2}$ pint	Single cream	300ml
3oz	Grated Parmesan cheese	75g
1oz	Dried breadcrumbs	25g

Sprinkle chicken breasts with a little salt. Heat butter in a frying pan and gently fry chicken for about 20 minutes, turning frequently, till tender and pale golden.

Preheat the grill.

Transfer chicken to a gratin dish.

Add cream to frying pan and cook over moderate heat, stirring to incorporate brown pieces left by the chicken. Add 2oz (50g) of the cheese and stir well. The sauce will thicken at once. Pour it over the chicken breasts.

Mix remaining cheese with breadcrumbs and sprinkle over chicken. Place dish under the grill and cook till surface is crisp and brown. Serve hot.

Chicken with cream and mushrooms

Overall timing 45 minutes

Freezing Suitable

To serve 4

3 oz	**Butter**	75 g
4	**Chicken pieces**	4
	Salt and pepper	
8 oz	**Mushrooms**	225 g
2 tbsp	**Plain flour**	2x15 ml
½ pint	**Chicken stock**	300 ml
½ pint	**Double cream**	300 ml

Melt 1½ oz (40 g) butter in a flameproof casserole and fry chicken till golden. Add salt, cover and cook gently for 20–30 minutes till tender.

Wipe and slice mushrooms, and add to chicken after 15 minutes.

Meanwhile, prepare sauce. Melt remaining butter in a saucepan, add flour and cook, stirring, for 2–3 minutes. Gradually stir in stock till smooth. Simmer, stirring, till thickened. Stir in cream and cook for 5 minutes, stirring occasionally. Season well.

Add sauce to chicken and serve hot, with saffron rice.

Deep-fried ginger chicken pieces

Overall timing 45 minutes plus marination

Freezing Not suitable

To serve 8

8	Chicken pieces	8
2	Garlic cloves	2
1	Large lemon	1
2 tbsp	Grated fresh ginger *or*	2x15 ml
1 tbsp	Ground ginger	15 ml
2 tbsp	Oil	2x15 ml
2 oz	Seasoned flour	50 g
1	Large egg	1
4 oz	Dried breadcrumbs	125 g
	Oil for frying	
	Lemon wedges	
	Sprigs of parsley	

Skin chicken pieces and prick all over with a skewer. Place in a large bowl. Peel and crush garlic. Squeeze juice from lemon. Combine garlic, lemon juice, ginger and oil and pour over chicken. Marinate for 3–4 hours, or overnight, turning once or twice.

Shake marinade off chicken pieces and roll in seasoned flour. Beat egg in a shallow dish. Dip chicken pieces in egg, then coat all over with breadcrumbs.

Heat ½ inch (1 cm) oil in a frying pan, add chicken pieces and fry for 10–15 minutes each side till golden.

Drain on kitchen paper and serve hot or cold, with lemon wedges and a parsley garnish.

Spaghetti with chicken sauce

Overall timing 1 hour

Freezing Suitable: cook spaghetti and almonds after reheating sauce

To serve 4

2	Thick streaky bacon rashers	2
12 oz	Boned chicken breasts	350 g
2 oz	Butter	50 g
2 tbsp	Oil	2x15 ml
1 lb	Ripe tomatoes	450 g
1	Garlic clove	1
2 tbsp	Tomato purée	2x15 ml
½ teasp	Sugar	2.5 ml
	Salt and pepper	
¼ pint	Dry white wine	150 ml
12 oz	Spaghetti	350 g
1 oz	Chopped almonds	25 g

Derind and dice the bacon. Wipe and trim the chicken, discarding skin. Cut the meat into strips. Heat half the butter and the oil in a flameproof casserole, add the bacon and chicken and fry for 5 minutes till browned all over.

Blanch, peel and chop the tomatoes. Add to the pan with the peeled and crushed garlic, tomato purée, sugar and salt and pepper. Add the wine and bring to the boil, stirring. Reduce the heat, cover the pan tightly and simmer for 20 minutes.

Meanwhile, cook the spaghetti in boiling salted water till just tender. Drain in a colander.

Melt remaining butter in the saucepan, add the almonds and fry over a high heat till golden. Return the spaghetti to the pan with half the tomato chicken sauce, toss lightly and adjust seasoning to taste. Place in a warmed serving dish.

Season remaining sauce, pour into a warmed sauceboat and serve separately.

Curried chicken with chicory

Overall timing 1 hour

Freezing Not suitable

To serve 4

4	Chicken pieces	4
	Salt and pepper	
4 teasp	Curry powder	4x5 ml
½ teasp	Paprika	2.5 ml
1 tbsp	Oil	15 ml
1 oz	Butter	25 g
4–6	Heads of chicory	4–6
7 teasp	Lemon juice	7x5 ml
	Pinch of sugar	
8 oz	Long grain rice	225 g
2 tbsp	Chopped parsley	2x15 ml
1 tbsp	Cornflour	15 ml
6 tbsp	Milk	6x15 ml
1 teasp	Soft brown sugar	5 ml

Wipe chicken. Mix 1 teasp (5 ml) salt and curry powder, pepper and paprika. Coat chicken pieces with mixture. Heat oil and butter in a frying pan. Add chicken and cook gently for about 30 minutes.

Meanwhile, place chicory in saucepan, cover with boiling water, add 6 teasp (6x5 ml) lemon juice, ¼ teasp (1.25 ml) salt and sugar. Cover and cook gently for 30 minutes.

Cook rice in boiling salted water for 15 minutes. Drain and mix with parsley. Press into 8 oiled ¼ pint (150 ml) dariole moulds.

Drain chicory and place on warmed serving dish with chicken pieces. Cover and keep warm. Unmould rice on to dish.

To make the sauce, sprinkle remaining curry powder on to fat in frying pan and stir to mix. Stir in 6 tbsp (6x15 ml) hot water. Blend cornflour with milk and add to pan with sugar and remaining lemon juice. Cook, stirring, for 7 minutes. Taste and correct seasoning if necessary. Strain over chicken and chicory.

Chinese chicken

Overall timing 45 minutes

Freezing Not suitable

To serve 4

4	Boned chicken breasts	4
1 tbsp	Cornflour	15 ml
1 tbsp	Soy sauce	15 ml
	Salt and pepper	
2 teasp	Finely chopped root ginger	2x5 ml
½ teasp	Caster sugar	2.5 ml
1	Garlic clove	1
4 oz	Dried mushrooms	125 g
4 tbsp	Oil	4x15 ml

Cut chicken breasts into small pieces with a sharp knife. Place chicken pieces in a bowl with 2 teasp (2x5 ml) of the cornflour, the soy sauce, pepper, ginger, sugar and peeled and crushed garlic. Mix well and leave for 15 minutes.

Wipe and thickly slice half the mushrooms, leaving the rest whole. Place in a saucepan, cover with boiling water and leave for 15 minutes. Drain mushrooms but save about 8 fl oz (220 ml) of the liquid and mix with the remaining cornflour and salt.

Heat oil in a frying pan. When hot add chicken and marinade and cook briskly for 10 minutes, stirring all the time. Add mushrooms and cornflour mixture. Stir-fry over a low heat for 5 minutes. Serve with plain boiled rice.

Turkey fries

Overall timing 40 minutes plus marination

Freezing Not suitable

To serve 8

4 tbsp	Oil	4x15 ml
3 tbsp	Lemon juice	3x15 ml
	Salt	
8x4 oz	Slices of turkey breast	8x125 g
4 teasp	Dijon mustard	4x5 ml
2	Eggs	2
8 oz	Fresh breadcrumbs	225 g
2 oz	Butter	50 g
	Chopped parsley	
	Lemon wedges	

Mix 2 tbsp (2x15 ml) of the oil with the lemon juice and a pinch of salt in a shallow dish. Add the turkey, mix well and leave to marinate for 1 hour.

Drain the turkey and pat dry on kitchen paper. Spread thinly with the mustard. Beat the eggs lightly on a plate and use to coat turkey. Dip turkey slices into the breadcrumbs, pressing them on gently.

Melt the butter and remaining oil in a frying pan and gently fry the turkey for about 10 minutes on each side, till tender and golden.

Drain on kitchen paper and arrange on a warmed dish. Garnish with chopped parsley and lemon wedges and serve immediately with a tomato and onion salad dressed with vinaigrette.

Stuffed drumsticks

Overall timing 2 hours

Freezing Not suitable

To serve 4

2x1 lb	Turkey drumsticks	2x450 g
	Salt and pepper	
4 oz	Smoked back bacon	125 g
	Rosemary leaves	
2 oz	Butter	50 g
2 teasp	Plain flour	2x5 ml
$\frac{1}{4}$ pint	Chicken stock	150 ml
4 tbsp	Dry vermouth	4x15 ml

Preheat the oven to 375°F (190°C) Gas 5.

Remove bone from drumsticks. Return drumsticks to their original shape, then season. Derind and chop bacon and stuff into cavities in the drumsticks. Close openings with skewers. Pierce the skin in several places and insert the rosemary leaves. Rub butter over drumsticks and place in a flameproof casserole. Cover and bake for about $1\frac{1}{4}$ hours.

Lift out the drumsticks and remove the skewers. Cut into thick slices, arrange on a serving dish and keep hot.

Add the flour to the casserole and stir over a low heat for 1 minute. Gradually add the stock and vermouth and bring to the boil, stirring. Simmer for 2 minutes then adjust the seasoning to taste.

Pour sauce over the turkey.

Devilled liver omelettes

Overall timing 20 minutes

Freezing Not suitable

To serve 4

4	Bacon rashers	4
8 oz	Chicken livers	225 g
	Salt and pepper	
2 tbsp	Plain flour	2x15 ml
4 oz	Mushrooms	125 g
3 oz	Butter	75 g
2 teasp	Tomato purée	2x5 ml
1 teasp	Worcestershire sauce	5 ml
1 teasp	French mustard	5 ml
12	Eggs	12
2 teasp	Chopped chives	2x5 ml

Derind and chop the bacon. Trim and chop the livers and toss in seasoned flour. Slice the mushrooms.

Melt 1 oz (25 g) of the butter in a saucepan, add the bacon and fry till light brown. Add the chicken livers and stir-fry till browned. Add the mushrooms, tomato purée, Worcestershire sauce, mustard and seasoning. Mix well, then cover and cook for 3 minutes.

Heat half the remaining butter in an omelette pan. Lightly beat the eggs with seasoning and add half to pan. Cook until almost set, then spoon half the liver mixture over and sprinkle with half the chives. Fold omelette and keep hot while you make second omelette in same way. Cut in half to serve.

Chicken liver pancakes

Overall timing 45 minutes

Freezing Suitable: add cream and cheese and bake from frozen, covered, allowing 30–40 minutes

To serve 4

4 oz	Chicken livers	125 g
8 oz	Button mushrooms	225 g
1	Small onion	1
2 oz	Butter	50 g
	Salt and pepper	
6	Slices of cooked ham	6
3 tbsp	Single cream	3x15 ml
	Grated nutmeg	
2 oz	Cheddar cheese	50 g
Pancakes		
5 oz	Plain flour	150 g
¼ teasp	Salt	1.25 ml
2	Eggs	2
½ pint	Beer	300 ml
	Oil for frying	

Chop chicken livers. Chop mushrooms. Peel and finely chop onion. Melt butter in a saucepan and gently fry mushrooms and onion for 5 minutes. Add chopped livers and fry for 3–4 minutes. Season with salt and pepper.

To make pancakes, sift flour and salt into a bowl and make a well in the centre. Add eggs and beer and beat to a smooth batter. Heat a little oil in an 8 inch (20 cm) pancake or frying pan and make 12 pancakes.

Preheat oven to 400°F (200°C) Gas 6.

Cut slices of ham in half. Place one half on each pancake. Divide liver mixture between pancakes, then roll them up. Place side by side in greased baking dish. Pour cream over and sprinkle with nutmeg and grated cheese.

Bake for 15–20 minutes, or grill for 5 minutes. Serve hot.

Chicken livers with herbs

Overall timing 10 minutes

Freezing Not suitable

To serve 6

1 lb	Chicken livers	450 g
2 oz	Butter	50 g
4	Fresh sage leaves	4
1	Fresh rosemary sprig	1
1	Bay leaf	1
	Salt and pepper	

Wash chicken livers and dry on kitchen paper. Cut them in half. Heat the butter in a frying pan and cook the livers for 2–3 minutes, stirring so that the livers brown all over.

Add the herbs and salt and pepper to taste. Cook for 1 minute, stirring. Serve with spinach or another green vegetable and fresh, sliced tomatoes.

Chicken and spinach pudding

Overall timing $1\frac{3}{4}$ hours

Freezing Not suitable

To serve 6

2lb	Spinach	900g
1lb	Cooked chicken meat (or chicken and turkey)	450g
1	Small onion	1
$1\frac{1}{2}$oz	Butter	40g
1 tbsp	Brandy (optional)	15ml
	Salt and pepper	
	Pinch of nutmeg	
$\frac{1}{4}$ teasp	Dried mixed herbs	1.25ml
4oz	Crustless bread	125g
	Milk	
1	Egg	1
2	Egg yolks	2
8fl oz	Single cream	250ml
4oz	Grated cheese	125g
	Dry breadcrumbs	

Preheat the oven to 350°F (180°C) Gas 4.

Wash the spinach, then cook with the water clinging to the leaves until tender. Drain well. Process in a blender or food processor till smooth.

Chop the chicken. Peel and chop the onion. Heat $\frac{1}{2}$oz (15g) butter in a frying pan and fry the onion until softened. Add the chicken and fry briefly. Pour over the brandy, heat and set alight. When the flames have died down, add seasoning, nutmeg and herbs. Cool.

Soak bread in milk and squeeze dry. Place in blender or food processor with chicken mixture and process till smooth. Beat in egg, egg yolks, cream, cheese and spinach. Adjust seasoning.

Use remaining butter to grease a deep 8 inch (20cm) mould and coat with dry breadcrumbs. Pour in chicken mixture. Bake for 1 hour or until knife inserted into pudding comes out clean. Turn out and serve hot, garnished with carrots.

Sautéed chicken livers in orange sauce

Overall timing 20 minutes

Freezing Not suitable

To serve 2

2	Oranges	2
5 tbsp	Sugar	5x15ml
2 teasp	Cornflour	2x5ml
1	Onion	1
2oz	Butter	50g
1 tbsp	Oil	15ml
7oz	Chicken livers	200g
	Salt and pepper	
$\frac{1}{2}$ teasp	Dried thyme	2.5ml

Pare rind from one orange very thinly, without any pith attached. Cut into julienne strips. Blanch strips in boiling water for 2 minutes. Drain and rinse in cold water.

Put rind back in saucepan, cover with $\frac{1}{2}$ inch (1cm) water and add sugar. Simmer till sugar is dissolved and rind is soft and transparent. Add more water if necessary.

Squeeze juice from both oranges. Stir in cornflour and mix well.

Peel and slice onion. Heat butter and oil in a frying pan and fry onion till golden. Remove from pan and set aside.

Add a little more oil to pan if necessary, and add chicken livers. Season with salt, pepper and thyme and stir-fry for about 2 minutes till well browned but still pink inside. Add onion and orange juice mixture. Stir well, then cover and simmer for 3–4 minutes.

Spoon liver mixture onto a bed of parsleyed rice and top with caramelized orange rind.

Spanish-style quail risotto

Overall timing 50 minutes

Freezing Not suitable

To serve 4		
1	Large onion	1
1	Garlic clove	1
1	Green pepper	1
6 tbsp	Oil	6x15 ml
8 oz	Long grain rice	225 g
1¼ pints	Water	700 ml
	Salt and pepper	
4	Ovenready quails	4
8 oz	Spicy sausages	225 g
4 oz	Frozen peas	125 g
1 teasp	Paprika	5 ml
½ teasp	Caster sugar	2.5 ml
2 oz	Grated Cheddar cheese	50 g
2	Large tomatoes	2
	Sprigs of parsley	

Peel and chop the onion; peel and crush the garlic. Wash, halve and deseed the pepper and slice thinly. Heat 2 tbsp (2x15 ml) of the oil in a flameproof casserole, add the onion, garlic and pepper and fry for 5 minutes.

Add the rice to the casserole and fry, stirring, for 2 minutes. Add the water, salt and pepper. Bring to the boil, cover and simmer for 15 minutes.

Meanwhile, heat the remaining oil in a frying pan and fry the quails till browned on all sides. Cover and cook for 10 minutes till tender.

Remove the skin from the sausages and slice thinly. Add to the rice with the peas, paprika and sugar. Cook for a further 5 minutes till the rice is tender. Stir the cheese into the risotto, taste and adjust seasoning.

Remove the quails from the pan and drain. Wash and halve the tomatoes, add to the pan and fry for 2–3 minutes each side.

Arrange the quails on the risotto with the tomatoes around the edge. Decorate with sprigs of parsley and serve immediately.

Stuffed boned rabbit

Overall timing 2 hours plus resting

Freezing Not suitable

To serve 6

4lb	Rabbit	1.8kg
1 tbsp	Dried rosemary	15ml
1 tbsp	Dried sage	15ml
	Salt and pepper	
6oz	Sliced prosciutto or cooked ham	175g
1	Garlic clove	1
2oz	Butter	50g
2 tbsp	Oil	2x15ml
½ pint	Dry white wine	300ml
	Chicken stock	

Place the rabbit, breast up, on a cutting board and make a cut lengthwise along the breast and belly. Using a very sharp knife, carefully remove all bones, so as to obtain one large piece of meat.

Mix rosemary and sage with salt and pepper to taste. Spread half herb mixture over meat, then cover with prosciutto or ham slices. Sprinkle with remaining herb mixture. Roll up meat and tie with string at 1 inch (2.5cm) intervals.

Peel garlic. Heat butter and oil in a flameproof casserole and sauté garlic till golden. Add rolled rabbit and brown on all sides. Discard garlic, then add wine and bring to the boil. Cover and simmer gently for 1¼ hours till rabbit is tender, adding stock to the casserole as necessary.

Remove rolled rabbit from casserole and let rest for 10 minutes before removing string and slicing. Serve with reduced cooking juices spooned over.

Chicken with lemon and olives

Overall timing $1\frac{1}{2}$ hours

Freezing Not suitable

To serve 4

1	Onion	1
1	Garlic clove	1
2	Thin-skinned lemons	2
2 tbsp	Chopped parsley	2x15 ml
$\frac{1}{2}$ teasp	Ground coriander	2.5 ml
	Salt and pepper	
$\frac{1}{4}$ teasp	Saffron	1.25 ml
3 lb	Ovenready chicken	1.4 kg
6 oz	Green olives	175 g
1 pint	Stock	600 ml
2 tbsp	Olive oil	2x15 ml

Preheat oven to 400°F (200°C) Gas 6.

Peel and chop onion. Peel and crush garlic. Wash and slice lemons. Place onion, garlic, parsley, coriander, salt, pepper and saffron in a roasting tin. Put chicken on top and arrange lemon slices and stoned olives around. Pour in stock and oil. Roast, basting frequently, for $1\frac{1}{4}$ hours or until meat is tender.

Place chicken on warmed serving dish and garnish with the lemon slices and olives. Boil cooking liquor till reduced by half. Taste and adjust seasoning. Spoon juices over chicken. Serve with rice or boiled new potatoes and a salad.

Tunisian chicken

Overall timing $2\frac{1}{4}$ hours

Freezing Not suitable

To serve 4

3lb	Ovenready chicken with giblets	1.4kg
	Salt and pepper	
5oz	Sweetcorn kernels	150g
3	Carrots	3
3	Medium potatoes	3
4	Tomatoes	4
4oz	Cheddar cheese	125g
1	Egg	1
2 tbsp	Breadcrumbs	2x15ml
1	Hard-boiled egg	1
1	Celery stalk	1
1	Sprig of parsley	1
2oz	Butter	50g
4 tbsp	Oil	4x15ml

Season chicken inside and out. Chop heart, liver and gizzard. Drain sweetcorn. Peel carrots and potatoes. Blanch, peel and quarter tomatoes.

Dice the cheese and mix with the sweetcorn, giblets, egg and breadcrumbs. Mash the hard-boiled egg with a fork and add to the mixture with seasoning. Mix well. Stuff the chicken with the mixture, then close opening.

Put carrots, potatoes and tomatoes into a flameproof casserole with celery and parsley. Cover with $2\frac{1}{2}$ pints (1.5 litres) water and bring to the boil. Lower heat and add chicken with half the butter. Cover and simmer for $1\frac{1}{2}$ hours.

Remove chicken and drain on kitchen paper. Strain cooking liquor and return to casserole. Purée vegetables and add to casserole. Heat soup through.

Heat remaining butter and oil in a frying pan. Put in whole chicken and brown evenly, turning it over with two spoons. Bring chicken and soup to table in separate dishes.

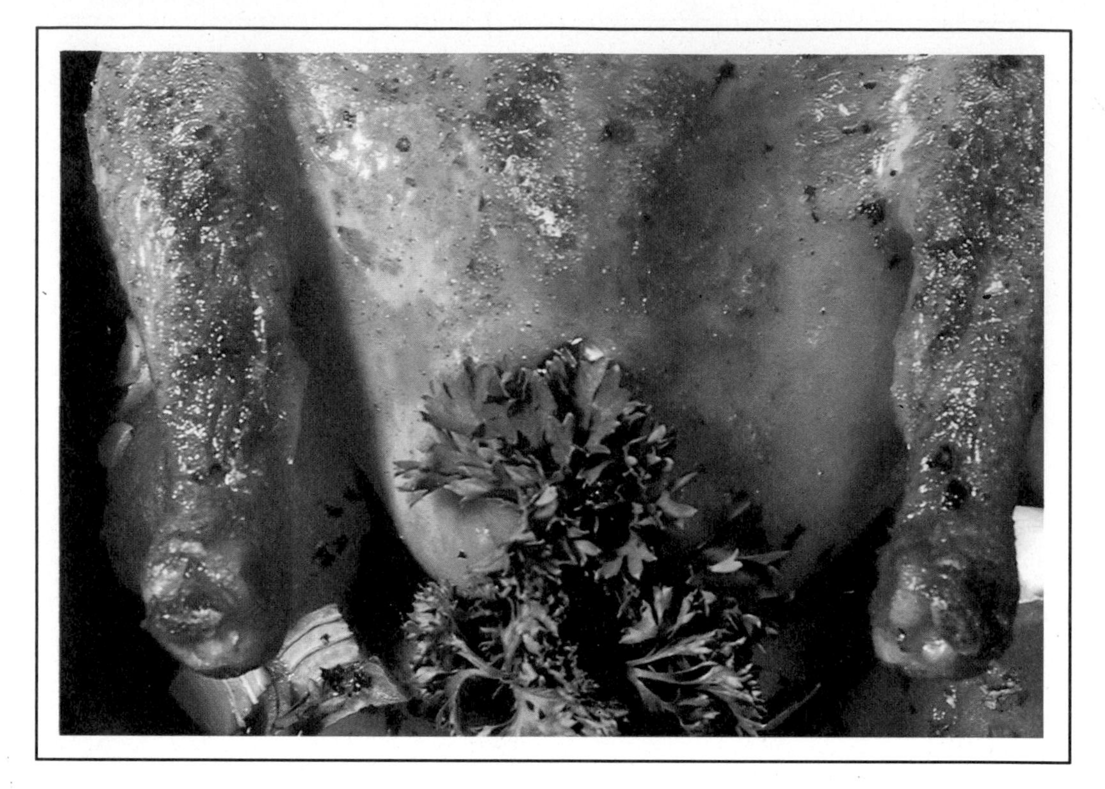

Braised chicken

Overall timing $1\frac{3}{4}$ hours

Freezing Not suitable

To serve 6

$3\frac{1}{2}$ lb	Ovenready chicken	1.6kg
	Salt and pepper	
2 teasp	Paprika	2x5ml
2oz	Butter	50g
$\frac{3}{4}$ pint	Chicken stock	400ml
3	Shallots	3
1lb	Small tomatoes	450g
1 tbsp	Chopped parsley	15ml
1 tbsp	Cornflour	15ml
3 tbsp	White wine	3x15ml

Preheat the oven to 400°F (200°C) Gas 6.

Wipe the chicken. Mix $\frac{1}{2}$ teasp (2.5ml) salt with the paprika and plenty of pepper. Sprinkle half the mixture inside the chicken and rub the rest into the skin. Heat the butter in a flameproof casserole, add the chicken and fry till browned all over. Add the stock, cover and cook in the oven for 1 hour.

Peel and finely chop the shallots. Blanch and peel the tomatoes. Arrange shallots and tomatoes round the chicken and sprinkle with parsley. Cover and cook for a further 20 minutes till the juices of the chicken run clear when the thickest part of the flesh is pierced with a skewer.

Lift the chicken out of the casserole and cut into 6 portions. Arrange on a warmed serving dish with tomatoes and shallots. Blend cornflour with wine and add to casserole. Bring to the boil, stirring constantly, then simmer for 3 minutes. Adjust the seasoning to taste, then pour over the chicken. Serve immediately with jacket baked potatoes.

Creole chicken

Overall timing $1\frac{1}{4}$ hours

Freezing Not suitable

To serve 4

3oz	Butter	75g
1	Garlic clove	1
4oz	Dried breadcrumbs	125g
1	Sugar lump	1
2	Limes	2
5 tbsp	Rum	5x15ml
	Grated nutmeg	
	Cayenne pepper	
	Salt and pepper	
5	Bananas	5
2oz	Mixed nuts	50g
1 tbsp	Desiccated coconut	15ml
3lb	Ovenready chicken	1.4kg
9fl oz	Chicken stock	250ml

Preheat the oven to 425°F (220°C) Gas 7.

Melt 2oz (50g) butter in a pan and brown peeled and lightly bruised garlic clove. Remove from pan and discard. Fry breadcrumbs till brown.

Rub sugar lump over rind of limes to absorb zest. Crush and add to pan. Squeeze limes and add 3 tbsp (3x15ml) juice to the pan with 1 tbsp (15ml) of rum, a pinch each of nutmeg and cayenne and seasoning. Stir for a few minutes, then remove from the heat and leave till breadcrumbs absorb liquid.

Peel and mash bananas. Mix in chopped nuts, coconut, remaining lime juice, 1 tbsp (15ml) of rum and seasoning.

Stuff breadcrumb mixture into one end of chicken and banana mixture into the other. Close both ends. Place in roasting tin and dot with remaining butter. Roast for 1 hour.

Remove chicken from tin, place on serving plate and keep warm. Pour chicken stock into tin and mix with pan juices. Bring to the boil and simmer for 2–3 minutes. Warm remaining rum, set alight and pour over the chicken. Serve with gravy and fried bananas.

Chicken in a brick

Overall timing 1½ hours

Freezing Not suitable

To serve 4–6

2	Onions	2
6	Celery stalks	6
1	Cooking apple	1
	Salt and pepper	
3lb	Ovenready chicken	1.4kg
6	Sage leaves	6
¼ pint	Dry cider	150ml
1	Red apple	1
½oz	Butter	15g
2 teasp	Cornflour	2x5ml
¼ pint	Soured cream	150ml

Soak the chicken brick in cold water for 15 minutes. Peel and slice onions. Thinly slice celery. Peel, core and chop cooking apple. Mix together and place in the base of the chicken brick. Season well.

Wipe the chicken and put the sage leaves inside. Place on top of vegetables. Pour cider over the chicken and cover with lid. Put into a cold oven, then set it to 450°F (230°C) Gas 8. Cook for 1¼ hours or until the chicken is tender.

Carefully core the red apple without peeling. Cut into thin slices. Heat the butter in a small pan and gently fry the apple slices until they are just tender but not yet browned.

Remove chicken from brick, place on serving plate and keep warm. Pour the juices and vegetables into a saucepan and bring to the boil. Blend the cornflour with 2 tbsp (2x15ml) water and stir into the pan. Boil for 1 minute. Remove from heat and add the soured cream. Adjust seasoning.

Pour sauce round chicken, garnish with apple slices and serve with jacket potatoes and parsleyed carrots.

Spanish chicken

Overall timing 2 hours

Freezing Not suitable

To serve 6

2oz	Rice	50g
4oz	Chicken livers	125g
1oz	Mushrooms	25g
6oz	Butter	175g
4lb	Ovenready chicken	1.8kg
½ pint	Hot chicken stock	300ml
1oz	Plain flour	25g
4floz	Single cream	120ml
Garnish		
5oz	Can of mushrooms	150g
2oz	Butter	50g
4oz	Cooked tongue	125g
4oz	Spicy sausage	125g
6	Cooked shortcrust pastry cases	6

To make stuffing, cook rice in boiling salted water for 15 minutes. Drain. Chop chicken livers. Slice mushrooms. Heat 2oz (50g) butter in a pan, add livers and mushrooms and cook for 5 minutes. Add rice. Season with salt. Stuff chicken with rice mixture and close up end. Season outside of bird with salt.

Heat 3oz (75g) butter in a flameproof casserole and brown chicken all over. Pour in stock, cover tightly and cook gently for 1½ hours.

To make garnish, drain canned mushrooms. Set aside 6. Heat butter in a small pan, add mushrooms, salt and pepper and cook gently for 5 minutes. Remove from heat and mix in chopped tongue and sausage.

Remove chicken from casserole and keep warm. Strain cooking liquor and measure out 9floz (250ml). Melt remaining butter in a small pan and stir in flour. Gradually stir in reserved liquor and cook for 5 minutes. Remove from heat, stir in cream and season.

Fill pastry cases. Pour a little sauce over each and garnish with reserved mushrooms. Arrange cases round chicken.

Chicken with juniper

Overall timing $1\frac{3}{4}$ hours

Freezing Not suitable

To serve 4

8	Juniper berries	8
1 teasp	Black peppercorns	5ml
1	Sprig of rosemary	1
2	Sage leaves	2
	Salt	
3lb	Ovenready chicken	1.4kg
4oz	Streaky bacon rashers	125g

Preheat oven to 350°F (180°C) Gas 4.

Crush the juniper berries and peppercorns in a mortar. Chop the rosemary and sage and mix with the juniper berries, peppercorns and salt to taste. Put 1 teasp (5ml) of the mixture inside the chicken. Spread remaining spice mixture over chicken. Cover chicken with bacon rashers.

Wrap chicken in foil and cook in oven for about $1\frac{1}{2}$ hours or till tender. Remove foil and bacon for the last 20 minutes to brown breast.

Stuffed roast chicken

Overall timing $2\frac{1}{4}$–$2\frac{3}{4}$ hours

Freezing Not suitable

To serve 6

$3\frac{1}{2}$ lb	Ovenready chicken	1.5 kg
8 oz	Stewing veal	225 g
4 oz	Pork fillet	125 g
4 oz	Sausagemeat	125 g
2	Eggs	2
1 oz	Grated Parmesan cheese	25 g
2 oz	Fresh breadcrumbs	50 g
1 teasp	Dried mixed herbs	5 ml
	Salt and pepper	
4 oz	Cooked ham	125 g
4 oz	Cooked tongue	125 g
1 tbsp	Pistachio nuts	15 ml
2 oz	Butter	50 g
4 tbsp	Brandy	4x15 ml

Put chicken on a chopping board, breast down, and cut open from neck to tail. Remove all bones except leg bones, keeping skin intact.

Chop veal and pork and mix with sausagemeat, eggs, cheese, breadcrumbs, herbs and seasoning. Cut ham and tongue into strips.

Preheat oven to 350°F (180°C) Gas 4.

Spread out chicken, skin down, and spread over half veal mixture. Cover with half ham and tongue strips and half pistachio nuts. Repeat layers. Fold skin of chicken over stuffing, tuck neck skin inside and sew carefully together with string.

Melt butter in a roasting pan, put in chicken sewed side down. Warm brandy, set alight and pour over chicken. Roast for $1\frac{1}{2}$–2 hours, basting occasionally.

Let rest for 10 minutes before slicing to serve.

Chicken in a basket

Overall timing 40 minutes

Freezing Not suitable

To serve 4

4x1 lb	Ovenready poussins	4x450 g
4 tbsp	Oil	4x15 ml
	Salt and pepper	
2 lb	Potatoes	900 g
	Oil for frying	
	Sprigs of parsley	
1	Onion	1

Preheat the oven to 400°F (200°C) Gas 6.

Place the poussins in roasting tin. Brush with oil and season well. Roast for 30 minutes, or until juices from the legs run clear when pierced with a skewer.

Meanwhile, peel potatoes and cut into thin, matchstick chips. Heat oil in a deep-fryer to 340°F (170°C). Fry chips for 3–5 minutes till golden. Drain well.

Arrange napkins in four small baskets. Place chips in folds of cloth. Place poussins in baskets. Garnish with parsley sprigs and onion rings. Eat with your fingers or a knife and fork if preferred.

Variation

To make barbecue-style poussins, mix together 4 tbsp (4x15 ml) tomato purée, 2 tbsp (2x15 ml) Worcestershire sauce, 2 tbsp (2x15 ml) oil, 1 peeled and crushed garlic clove and seasoning. Spread over poussins, cover with foil and roast for 40 minutes. Serve as above.

Grilled poussins

Overall timing $1\frac{1}{4}$ hours

Freezing Not suitable

To serve 4

4x12 oz	Ovenready poussins	4x350 g
4 tbsp	Coarse-grain mustard	4x15 ml
	Cayenne pepper	
2 teasp	Worcestershire sauce	2x5 ml
1 teasp	Vinegar	5 ml
6 tbsp	Oil	6x15 ml
	Salt and pepper	

Wipe the poussins and trim off the ends of the legs. Place 1 breast down on a board. Using poultry shears, cut along one side of the backbone, then along the other side to remove it cleanly from the body. Turn the poussin breast side up and open out. Using a rolling-pin or the heel of the hand, press down on the breast to break the ribs and flatten the bird. Flatten the others in the same way.

Tuck the wing tips under the bird. Fold the legs so they lie as flat as possible. Push a skewer through the wing, then the breast and the other wing. Skewer the legs in the same way so the birds are kept flat. Line the grill rack with foil and arrange the poussins on it skin side down.

Mix the mustard, pinch of cayenne, Worcestershire sauce, vinegar, oil and seasoning together. Brush half over the birds and leave to marinate for 15 minutes.

Preheat the grill.

Grill the poussins for 10 minutes, 3 inches (7.5 cm) below heat. Turn poussins carefully with skewers and brush with remaining marinade. Grill for a further 8–10 minutes till tender. Place the poussins on a bed of rice, mixed with bacon and diced green pepper, and serve immediately.

Boiled stuffed capon

Overall timing $2\frac{1}{2}$ hours

Freezing Not suitable

To serve 6

5lb	Ovenready capon with liver	2.3kg
2oz	Pork fillet	50g
2oz	Cooked ham	50g
2oz	Fresh breadcrumbs	50g
2 tbsp	Chopped parsley	2x15ml
2	Egg yolks	2
	Grated nutmeg	
	Salt and pepper	
	Chicken stock	
1	Celery stalk	1
1	Leek	1
1	Potato	1
1	Carrot	1

Finely chop the liver, pork and ham. Mix these with the breadcrumbs, parsley, egg yolks, a pinch of nutmeg and seasoning. Stuff capon and sew up opening. Wrap capon in a clean dish towel or muslin and tie securely at both ends.

Place the wrapped capon in a saucepan, cover with stock and bring slowly to the boil. Skim off the scum.

Meanwhile, trim and slice or chop the celery and leek. Peel and slice or chop the potato and carrot.

Add the vegetables to the pan and simmer gently for about 2 hours or until the capon is tender.

Unwrap the capon and let rest for 10 minutes before carving.

Roast capon with aubergines

Overall timing $2\frac{1}{2}$ hours

Freezing Not suitable

To serve 6

6lb	Ovenready capon with giblets	2.6kg
$\frac{1}{2}$ pint	Water	300ml
	Salt and pepper	
1 tbsp	Dried tarragon	15ml
3oz	Butter	75g
9oz	Aubergines	250g
$1\frac{1}{2}$lb	Tomatoes	700g
8oz	Large mushrooms	225g
	Parsley	
4 tbsp	Oil	4x15ml
	Plain flour	
2 tbsp	Madeira	2x15ml

Preheat oven to 400°F (200°C) Gas 6.

Cover giblets with water and bring to boil. Simmer for 15 minutes then strain, reserving liquid. Rub inside of capon with salt, pepper and tarragon. Smear outside with butter. Place capon on a rack in a roasting tin, pour in giblet stock and roast for 2 hours, basting frequently.

Meanwhile, cut aubergines into $\frac{1}{4}$ inch (6mm) thick slices. Sprinkle with salt and set aside for 30 minutes. Wash and dry tomatoes. Slice mushrooms. Chop some of the parsley.

Heat 2 tbsp (2x15ml) oil in a frying pan and brown mushrooms for 2–3 minutes. Season with salt and pepper and add 2 tbsp (2x15ml) chopped parsley. Mix together, lower heat and cook for about 5 minutes. Remove from pan and keep warm.

Rinse aubergine slices, wipe dry and lightly flour. Pour a little more oil into frying pan. Add aubergines and fry for 4 minutes on each side. Remove from pan and keep warm. Add a little more oil to pan and gently cook tomatoes for 5 minutes on each side. Keep warm.

When the capon is cooked, turn off oven and leave capon to "rest" for about 20 minutes. Pour cooking juices into a saucepan and bring to the boil. Skim off fat, then simmer for 5–10 minutes. Stir in Madeira.

Serve capon with tomatoes, aubergines and mushrooms and garnish dish with parsley. Serve gravy separately.

Canadian wild rice stuffed duck

Overall timing 5¼ hours plus soaking

Freezing Not suitable

To serve 4–6

½ oz	Dried mushrooms	15 g
2 oz	Butter	50g
6 oz	Chopped onion	175 g
4 oz	Wild rice	125 g
¾ pint	Chicken stock	450 ml
	Salt and pepper	
5 lb	Ovenready duck	2.3 kg
2 tbsp	Plain flour	2x15 ml
2 tbsp	Brandy	2x15 ml
¼ teasp	Dried thyme	1.25 ml
2 tbsp	Double cream	2x15 ml

Place the dried mushrooms in a small bowl with 6 fl oz (170 ml) of water and soak for 2 hours. Drain, reserve soaking liquor and chop mushrooms coarsely.

Melt butter in frying pan, add 2 oz (50 g) onion and cook till soft. Add rice and stir to coat in butter. Pour in 8 fl oz (220 ml) of stock and season. Bring to boil, cover tightly and simmer for 30–45 minutes. Check from time to time and if too dry, add more stock.

Stuff duck with rice and stand on wire rack in roasting tin. Prick all over and rub skin with salt and pepper. Roast for 1¾ hours or until juices run clear when thigh is pierced with a fine skewer. Transfer duck to a warm dish, cover and keep warm.

Pour away all but 2 tbsp (2x15 ml) of the pan juices and add remaining onion. Cook till soft. Add flour and mix well. Stir in remaining stock, reserved liquor from mushrooms, brandy and thyme and cook, stirring, till sauce boils and thickens. Remove from heat and stir in cream.

Strain sauce through a fine sieve into a small saucepan, pressing down hard on onions to extract juice before discarding pulp. Add reserved mushrooms and heat through. Taste and adjust seasoning, then pour sauce into sauce boat and serve with the duck.

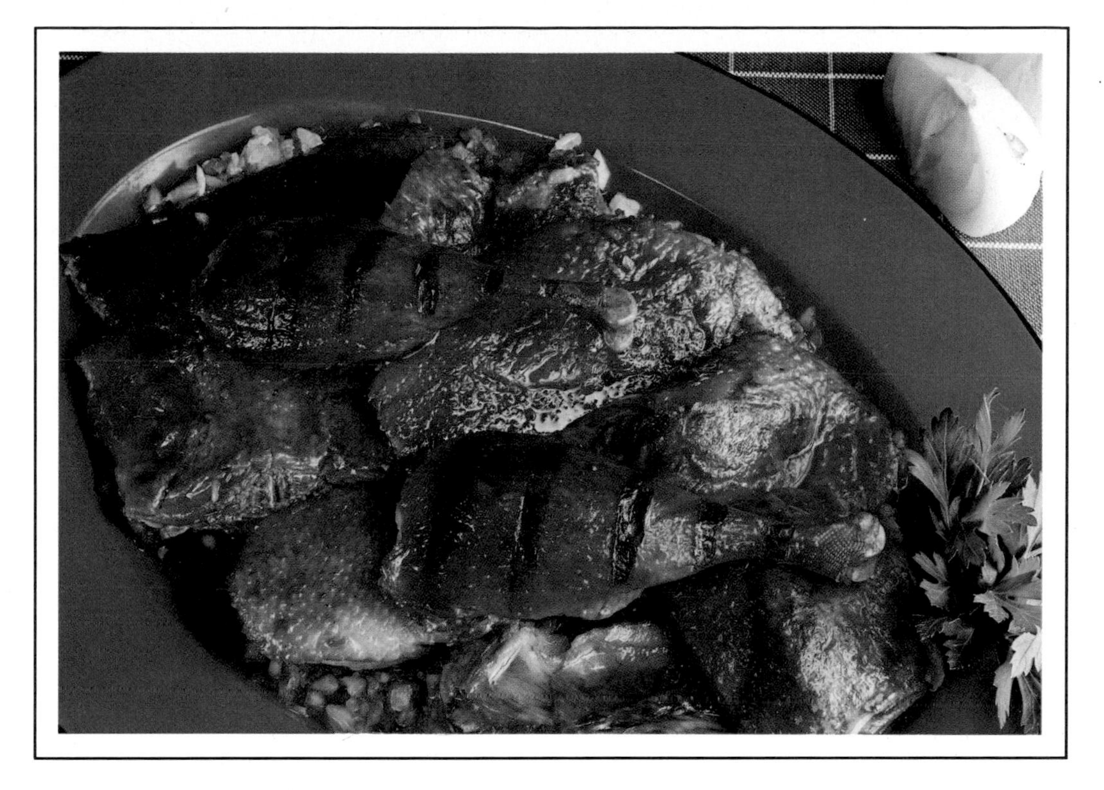

Rouen duck

Overall timing $1\frac{1}{4}$ hours

Freezing Not suitable

To serve 4

4lb	Ovenready duck	1.8kg
	Salt and pepper	
4	Shallots or onions	4
2oz	Butter	50g
2 tbsp	Plain flour	2x15ml
$\frac{1}{2}$ pint	Chicken stock	300ml
$\frac{1}{4}$ pint	Red wine	150ml

Preheat oven to 400°F (200°C) Gas 6.

Prick duck all over and place on a wire rack in a roasting tin. Rub salt into skin and roast for 1 hour. Cut duck into portions with game or kitchen scissors. Keep portions warm.

Peel and chop shallots or onions. Heat butter in a large saucepan, add shallots or onions and cook till transparent. Sprinkle with flour, salt and pepper, then gradually add the stock. Cook gently for 2–3 minutes, stirring, then add the wine and cook for a further 10 minutes or till the sauce thickens.

Put onion sauce on to warm serving plate, put duck on top and serve.

Marinated duck

Overall timing $1\frac{1}{2}$ hours plus marination

Freezing Not suitable

To serve 4

1	Onion	1
1	Garlic clove	1
1oz	Green olives	25g
2	Canned sardines	2
1 pint	Red wine	600ml
$\frac{1}{2}$ teasp	Dried rosemary	2.5ml
$\frac{1}{2}$ teasp	Dried oregano	2.5ml
$\frac{1}{2}$ teasp	Dried basil	2.5ml
4lb	Ovenready duck	1.8kg
	Salt and pepper	
2 tbsp	Oil	2x15ml
1	Egg yolk	1
	Mustard cress	

Peel and chop the onion and garlic. Stone and chop olives. Chop sardines. Put into a shallow dish with the wine and herbs. Mix well together. Wipe duck. Cut into 8 pieces with game or kitchen scissors. Place duck joints in marinade. Leave for 2 hours.

Remove duck from marinade and dry on kitchen paper. Prick joints with a fork and sprinkle with salt and pepper. Heat the oil in a large saucepan, add duck pieces a few at a time and quickly brown on all sides. Pour off fat. Add marinade to pan, cover and simmer gently for about 1 hour or until the duck is very tender.

Remove duck from pan with a draining spoon, place on warmed serving plate and keep hot. Skim off fat and strain pan juices. Beat the egg yolk with 2 tbsp (2x15ml) of the pan juices, then stir into the pan over very gentle heat.

Pour sauce over duck pieces. Garnish with mustard cress and serve with baked tomatoes and long macaroni.

Duck with mustard sauce

Overall timing 2 hours

Freezing Not suitable

To serve 4

3½ lb	Ovenready duck	1.6 kg
1	Bouquet garni	1
	Salt and pepper	
1	Lettuce	1
1 lb	Peas	450 g
2 tbsp	Lemon juice	2x15 ml
2	Egg yolks	2
4 tbsp	Single cream	4x15 ml
1 teasp	Dijon mustard	5 ml

Preheat the oven to 400°F (200°C) Gas 6.

Wipe duck and insert bouquet garni. Season and prick all over with a fork. Place on wire rack in roasting tin and roast for 1–1¼ hours or until duck is cooked.

Wash and trim lettuce. Put into a pan with the peas and lemon juice. Cover tightly and cook over a gentle heat for about 20 minutes (10 minutes if using frozen peas).

Place vegetables on serving dish. Remove duck from roasting tin and cut into portions with game scissors. Arrange on top of vegetables and keep hot.

Strain pan juices. Beat together the egg yolks, cream and mustard in a small saucepan. Gradually stir in the strained stock and heat gently until slightly thickened. Spoon over the duck and serve immediately.

Roast goose

Overall timing $2\frac{1}{2}$ hours

Freezing Not suitable

To serve 6–8

2 oz	Butter	50 g
1 teasp	Dried sage	5 ml
1 teasp	Dried rosemary	5 ml
$7\frac{1}{2}$ lb	Ovenready goose	3.4 kg
	Salt and pepper	
$\frac{1}{4}$ pint	Dry white wine	150 ml

Preheat oven to 475°F (240°C) Gas 9.

Mix $\frac{1}{2}$ oz (15 g) butter with sage and rosemary and place inside goose. Truss goose. Sprinkle outside of goose liberally with salt and pepper and dot with remaining butter. Place in a roasting tin.

Roast goose until browned, then reduce oven temperature to 375°F (190°C) Gas 5. Pour wine over goose. Continue roasting, pricking occasionally with a fork to let fat escape and basting with wine in tin, for about 2 hours.

Let goose rest for 10 minutes before untrussing and carving.

Guinea fowl with vegetables

Overall timing 1¼ hours

Freezing Not suitable

To serve 4

8oz	Button onions	225g
2lb	Potatoes	900g
2	Ovenready guinea fowl	2
	Salt and pepper	
3oz	Butter	75g
8oz	Streaky bacon	225g
8oz	Button mushrooms	225g
2 tbsp	Chopped parsley	2x15ml

Peel onions and potatoes and cut potatoes into chunks. Cook them in boiling water for 5 minutes, drain and dry thoroughly.

Season guinea fowl inside and out with salt and pepper. Heat 2oz (50g) of butter in a flameproof casserole and brown the birds on all sides, then remove from dish and set aside.

Chop the bacon and sauté in the casserole with onions and potatoes until golden brown. Season with salt and pepper. Return the guinea fowl to the dish, cover and cook for 40–50 minutes over medium heat.

Meanwhile, wipe mushrooms. Heat remaining butter in frying pan and fry the mushrooms until golden. Add them to the casserole 5 minutes before the end of cooking.

Place guinea fowl on a warm serving dish, arrange vegetables around and sprinkle with parsley.

Partridge with grapes and bacon

Overall timing 1 hour

Freezing Not suitable

To serve 4

2	**Ovenready partridges**	2
1	**Garlic clove**	1
	Fresh rosemary	
	Salt and pepper	
4	**Streaky bacon rashers**	4
3oz	**Butter**	75g
7fl oz	**Dry white wine**	200ml
12oz	**Seedless white grapes**	350g
1 tbsp	**Cornflour**	15ml

Preheat the oven to 425°F (220°C) Gas 7.

Wipe the partridges. Peel and finely slice garlic. Put a few garlic slices, a sprig of rosemary, salt and pepper inside each bird. Wrap 2 bacon rashers round each one and secure with wooden cocktail sticks. Place partridges in casserole with 2oz (50g) of the butter. Season with salt and pepper and sprinkle with a little extra rosemary. Cover and roast for 15 minutes.

Bring 3fl oz (90ml) of the wine to the boil in a pan. Turn partridges over and baste with the wine. Roast for a further 15 minutes.

Meanwhile, blanch the grapes in boiling water for 2 minutes, then remove skins with a sharp knife.

Remove partridges from casserole, place on serving plate and keep warm. Blend cornflour with remaining wine and stir into cooking liquor. Bring to the boil, stirring, and cook for a few minutes until sauce thickens. Add remaining butter and peeled grapes to sauce, stir for 1 minute, then remove from heat immediately.

Remove bacon rashers and cut partridges in half with game scissors. Arrange bacon over partridge halves, pour sauce over and serve immediately with creamed or boiled potatoes and a watercress salad.

Stuffed braised pigeons

Overall timing $1\frac{3}{4}$ hours

Freezing Not suitable

To serve 4

2	Large ovenready pigeons with livers	2
2 oz	Cooked ham	50 g
2 oz	Butter	50 g
4 tbsp	Brandy	4x15 ml
2 oz	Fresh breadcrumbs	50 g
1	Egg yolk	1
2 tbsp	Grated cheese	2x15 ml
1 tbsp	Chopped parsley	15 ml
	Salt and pepper	
4	Streaky bacon rashers	4
1	Bay leaf	1
	Chicken stock	

Mince livers with ham. Heat 1 oz (25 g) butter in a frying pan, add livers and ham and fry till livers are browned. Warm 2 tbsp (2x15 ml) brandy, set alight and add to pan. Mix well and remove from the heat. Add breadcrumbs, egg yolk, cheese, parsley and seasoning and combine thoroughly.

Stuff pigeons with mixture and truss. Place 2 bacon rashers on each bird and tie on with string.

Melt remaining butter in a flameproof casserole. Add pigeons and brown on all sides. Add remaining brandy, warm it and set alight. When flames die down, add bay leaf and enough stock to cover bottom of casserole. Cover and cook gently for about 1 hour till pigeons are tender, adding more stock as necessary.

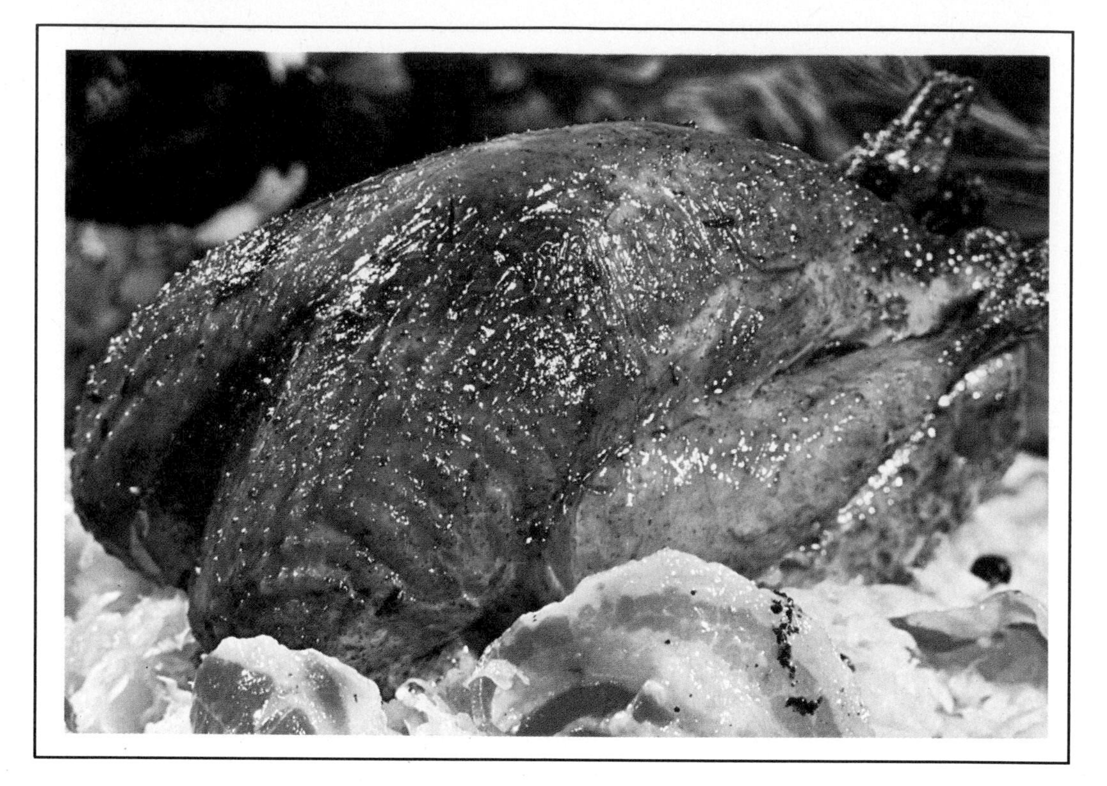

Pheasant with sauerkraut

Overall timing $1\frac{1}{2}$ hours

Freezing Not suitable

To serve 4

	Salt and pepper	
$2\frac{1}{2}$ lb	Ovenready pheasant	1.1kg
1	Cooking apple	1
10	Thin streaky bacon rashers	10
1oz	Butter	25g
$\frac{1}{4}$ pint	Cider	150ml
2lb	Sauerkraut	900g

Preheat oven to 400°F (200°C) Gas 6.

Season pheasant inside. Peel apple and place inside pheasant. Derind and stretch 6 of the bacon rashers, wrap around pheasant and secure with wooden cocktail sticks. Place in a roasting tin with butter and cider and cover with foil. Bake for 40 minutes, basting occasionally.

Remove roasting tin from oven and discard the foil. Arrange sauerkraut round pheasant, top with remaining bacon and return to oven to cook for 20 minutes. Serve with sauté potatoes.

Pheasant in rich sauce

Overall timing $1\frac{1}{4}$ hours

Freezing Not suitable

To serve 4

$2\frac{1}{2}$ lb	Ovenready pheasant	1.1 kg
6	Streaky bacon rashers	6
2	Shallots	2
3 oz	Butter	75 g
2 tbsp	Plain flour	2x15 ml
$\frac{1}{4}$ pint	Game stock	150 ml
$\frac{1}{4}$ pint	Dry white wine	150 ml
	Salt and pepper	
	Fried croûtons	
	Sprigs of parsley	

Preheat the oven to 450°F (230°C) Gas 8.

Cover the pheasant with the bacon and roast for 10 minutes. Reduce the oven temperature to 400°F (200°C) Gas 6 and roast for a further 20 minutes. Remove from the oven. Lift off and reserve the bacon.

Peel and thinly slice the shallots. Cut the pheasant into 6 even-size pieces. Heat the butter in a flameproof casserole and fry the shallots for 5 minutes. Add pheasant and cook for 5 minutes. Sprinkle the flour over and cook over high heat for 3 minutes, till brown. Gradually add the stock and wine. Dice reserved bacon and add to the casserole. Bring to the boil, stirring. Season, then cover and simmer for 10 minutes.

Arrange in a warmed serving dish and garnish with fried croûtons and sprigs of parsley. Serve immediately.

Chicken sautéed with tomatoes

Overall timing 45 minutes

Freezing Suitable

To serve 6

6	Onions	6
4 tbsp	Olive oil	4x15 ml
6	Chicken pieces	6
2	Garlic cloves	2
1 teasp	Dried thyme	5 ml
14 oz	Can of crushed tomatoes	400 g
7 fl oz	Red or white wine	200 ml
	Salt and pepper	
1	Lemon	1
10	Black olives	10
2 tbsp	Chopped parsley	2x15 ml

Peel and quarter onions. Heat 2 tbsp (2x15 ml) oil in a frying pan. Add onions and fry gently till soft and golden. Remove from pan and set aside.

Add remaining oil to pan, then add chicken pieces and sauté briskly till browned on all sides.

Return onions to pan. Peel and crush garlic. Add garlic to pan with thyme, tomatoes, wine and seasoning. Cook gently for 20–30 minutes, stirring occasionally, till chicken is tender.

Add a squeeze of lemon juice and the olives. Serve hot, sprinkled with parsley.

Sautéed chicken wings with clams

Overall timing 40 minutes

Freezing Suitable

To serve 4

2 tbsp	Olive oil	2x15ml
2oz	Butter	50g
2lb	Chicken wings	900g
1lb 12oz	Can of tomatoes	794g
1 tbsp	Dried chillies	15ml
1 teasp	Dried thyme	5ml
10oz	Can of clams	275g
4 tbsp	Chopped parsley	4x15ml
2 tbsp	Capers	2x15ml

Heat oil and butter in a large frying pan. Add chicken wings and brown on all sides.

Drain tomatoes and add to chicken with chillies and thyme. Simmer for 15 minutes, stirring occasionally.

Drain clams, reserving juice. Add clams to chicken with 2 tbsp (2x15ml) juice. Cook for a further 3 minutes.

Serve hot, sprinkled with parsley and capers.

Chicken, leek and rice casserole

Overall timing $1\frac{3}{4}$ hours

Freezing Suitable

To serve 4

4	Large leeks	4
2oz	Butter	50g
1 pint	Milk	600ml
4	Chicken pieces	4
6oz	Long-grain rice	175g
	Salt	

Preheat oven to 300°F (150°C) Gas 2.

Trim leeks and cut into 1 inch (2.5cm) pieces. Wash well. Melt 1oz (25g) butter in a frying pan and cook leeks till soft. Set aside.

Heat milk almost to boiling point. Set aside.

Grease a large casserole with remaining butter. Arrange leeks, chicken and rice in layers in casserole and season with salt. Pour in hot milk. Cover tightly and cook in the oven for $1\frac{1}{2}$ hours till chicken is tender and rice has absorbed milk.

Chicken goulash

Overall timing 40 minutes

Freezing Suitable

To serve 4

2 tbsp	Oil	2x15 ml
8	Small chicken pieces	8
2	Onions	2
1 tbsp	Paprika	15 ml
	Salt	
4 tbsp	Chicken stock	4x15 ml
2	Red or green peppers	2
½ pint	Soured cream	300 ml
1 tbsp	Plain flour	15 ml

Heat oil in a flameproof casserole and brown chicken pieces on all sides. Remove from the pot and set aside.

Peel and chop onions. Add to casserole and cook till browned lightly. Stir in paprika and salt. Add stock and stir well.

Deseed and chop peppers. Add to casserole. Return chicken to casserole and cover tightly. Cook very gently for 30 minutes, stirring occasionally, till chicken is tender.

Transfer chicken to a warmed serving dish and keep hot. Mix soured cream with flour. Add to casserole, stirring well, and cook till sauce is thickened. Spoon sauce over chicken.

Turkey and potato scallop

Overall timing 45 minutes

Freezing Suitable

To serve 8

3 oz	Butter	75 g
3 tbsp	Oil	3x15 ml
3 lb	Turkey escalopes	1.4 kg
4 fl oz	Chicken stock	120 ml
	Salt and pepper	
2 lb	Onions	900 g
2 lb	Potatoes	900 g
$1\frac{1}{2}$ pints	Milk	900 ml
$\frac{1}{2}$ teasp	Grated nutmeg	2.5 ml
1	Garlic clove	1
1 teasp	Dried mixed herbs	5 ml
$\frac{1}{4}$ pint	Single cream	150 ml
2 tbsp	Chopped parsley	2x15 ml

Heat $1\frac{1}{2}$ oz (40 g) butter and 2 tbsp (2x15 ml) oil in a frying pan and quickly fry escalopes till they change colour. Remove from the pan and set aside.

Deglaze pan with half the stock, stir well and pour over escalopes. Season well.

Preheat oven to 400°F (200°C) Gas 6.

Peel and thinly slice onions. Heat remaining butter and oil in frying pan and fry onions gently, covered, for 20 minutes till soft and golden. Season well.

Meanwhile, peel and thinly slice potatoes. Cook in milk with nutmeg and a little salt for 15–20 minutes till tender. Do not overcook. Drain, reserving milk.

Peel garlic and rub clove round inside of a gratin dish. Make layers of onions and turkey in dish and sprinkle with herbs. Add remaining stock and juices from turkey. Arrange potato slices on top and pour over enough reserved milk to moisten dish well. Dribble cream over all. Bake for 15–20 minutes.

Preheat grill. Brown top of dish under grill, and sprinkle with parsley before serving.

Sweet and sour chicken

Overall timing $1\frac{1}{4}$ hours

Freezing Not suitable

To serve 4–6

8	Chicken pieces	8
	Salt and pepper	
3 tbsp	Oil	3x15 ml
9 fl oz	Hot chicken stock	250 ml
8 oz	Can of pineapple pieces	227 g
2 oz	Butter	50 g
4 oz	Flaked almonds	125 g
2	Bananas	2
1	Orange	1
4 oz	Cocktail cherries	110 g
2 tbsp	Mild curry powder	2x15 ml
2 tbsp	Cornflour	2x15 ml
4 fl oz	Plain yogurt or single cream	113 ml

Preheat oven to 375°F (190°C) Gas 5. Wash and dry chicken pieces. Rub with salt and pepper. Heat the oil in flameproof casserole and brown chicken on all sides. Put the chicken in the oven and cook, uncovered, for 40 minutes. Baste with stock frequently.

Meanwhile, drain the pineapple and save the juice. Melt butter in a saucepan, add almonds and cook till golden brown. Peel and slice bananas and orange and add to almonds with drained cherries and pineapple pieces. Turn mixture over, heat through then remove from heat.

Remove casserole from the oven. Place the chicken pieces on a warm serving dish. Cover with the fruit and almond mixture and keep warm. Combine any remaining chicken stock with chicken juices and pineapple juice. Make up to $\frac{3}{4}$ pint (400 ml) with water.

In saucepan, mix curry powder and cornflour together. Gradually stir in measured liquid. Bring to the boil, stirring, and cook for 1–2 minutes. Remove from heat and stir in yogurt or cream. Pour some sauce over chicken; put remainder in a sauceboat.

Ragoût of chicken in red wine vinegar

Overall timing 50 minutes

Freezing Suitable

To serve 8

1	Small onion	1
2	Garlic cloves	2
6 tbsp	Olive oil	6x15 ml
8	Chicken pieces	8
4 tbsp	Plain flour	4x15 ml
4 fl oz	Red wine vinegar	120 ml
½ pint	Chicken stock	300 ml
1 teasp	Dried thyme	5 ml
	Salt and pepper	
24	Small pickling onions	24
2 oz	Butter	50 g
2 tbsp	Sugar	2x15 ml
1 lb	Carrots	450 g
4 tbsp	Chopped parsley	4x15 ml

Peel and finely chop onion and garlic. Heat 2 tbsp (2x15 ml) oil in a flameproof casserole and fry onion and garlic till soft.

Coat chicken pieces with flour. Add remaining oil to casserole, then fry chicken pieces till well browned on all sides. Remove chicken from pot and set aside.

Add vinegar to casserole and stir well. Cook till reduced by half. Return chicken to casserole and add stock, thyme and seasoning. Cover and simmer for about 20 minutes.

Meanwhile, peel pickling onions. Melt butter in a frying pan, add onions with about 4 fl oz (120 ml) water, the sugar and seasoning, and fry till onions are tender and glazed.

Peel and slice carrots and cook in boiling salted water till just tender. Drain.

Add carrots and onions to casserole. Simmer for a further 10 minutes till chicken is tender. Serve sprinkled with parsley.

Chicken with rosemary

Overall timing 1 hour

Freezing Suitable

To serve 8

6 oz	Butter	175 g
2 tbsp	Oil	2x15 ml
8	Chicken pieces	8
1 pint	Chicken stock	600 ml
10	Sprigs of rosemary	10
$\frac{1}{4}$ teasp	Dried thyme	1.25 ml
	Salt and pepper	
2 oz	Plain flour	50 g
$\frac{1}{2}$ pint	Double cream	300 ml
8 oz	Carrots	225 g
8 oz	Button mushrooms	225 g

Heat 2 oz (50 g) butter with the oil in a flameproof casserole. Add chicken pieces and brown on all sides. Remove from the pot and set aside.

Add stock to casserole and stir well to mix in sediments from bottom. Add 8 sprigs of rosemary, the thyme and seasoning. Simmer for 20 minutes. Strain and set aside.

Melt 2 oz (50 g) butter in a clean casserole, stir in flour and cook for 1 minute. Gradually stir in stock mixture and simmer till thickened. Stir in cream.

Add chicken pieces to sauce, with their juices. Simmer for about 20 minutes, stirring occasionally, till chicken is tender. Add more stock if sauce becomes too thick.

Meanwhile, peel and slice carrots. Cook in boiling salted water till just tender. Drain. Fry mushrooms in remaining butter.

About 5 minutes before chicken is ready, add carrots and mushrooms to casserole.

Break up remaining 2 sprigs of rosemary and add to casserole. Serve with rice.

Indian-style chicken

Overall timing $1\frac{1}{4}$ hours

Freezing Suitable: add cream after thawing

To serve 4

1	Onion	1
1oz	Butter	25g
1 tbsp	Oil	15ml
3lb	Chicken pieces	1.4kg
2 tbsp	Mild curry powder	2x15ml
$\frac{1}{2}$ pint	Chicken stock	300ml
1	Garlic clove	1
2 tbsp	Lemon juice	2x15ml
	Salt	
	Cayenne pepper	
2 tbsp	Single cream	2x15ml

Peel and chop onion. Heat butter and oil in a flameproof casserole and cook onions till transparent. Add chicken pieces, a few at a time, and brown on all sides. Sprinkle chicken with curry powder and pour in stock. Add peeled and crushed garlic, lemon juice and a pinch each of salt and cayenne pepper. Cover and simmer for 35 minutes over a low heat.

Add cream and cook gently for 10 minutes. Do not boil. Serve with plain boiled rice and side dishes of apple slices, cucumber sprinkled with salt and grated fresh coconut, if liked.

Maharajah's chicken

Overall timing 20 minutes

Freezing Not suitable

To serve 2

1–2	Large garlic cloves	1–2
1	Large onion	1
1-inch	Piece of fresh root ginger	2.5-cm
1	Lemon	1
2 oz	Butter	50 g
10 oz	Boneless chicken breasts	275 g
	Salt	
1 teasp	Turmeric	5 ml
2 tbsp	Chopped fresh coriander	2x15 ml

Peel garlic, onion and ginger. Squeeze juice from lemon. Using a food processor or blender, process garlic, ginger and one-quarter of the onion to a fine mush with half the lemon juice. Set aside.

Slice remaining onion thinly. Melt butter in a frying pan and fry sliced onion till soft and beginning to brown.

Meanwhile, cut chicken into $\frac{3}{4}$ inch (2 cm) cubes, discarding all skin. Add chicken cubes to onion and cook, stirring, till chicken changes colour. Add salt, turmeric and garlic mush and stir well. Cook, stirring frequently, about 5 minutes.

Add remaining lemon juice, and serve sprinkled with chopped coriander.

Mexican-style chicken

Overall timing 1½ hours plus soaking

Freezing Not suitable

To serve 4

4oz	Dried haricot beans	125g
6 tbsp	Oil	6x15ml
4	Chicken pieces	4
2	Onions	2
2	Garlic cloves	2
1 teasp	Chilli powder	5ml
8fl oz	Hot chicken stock	225ml
8oz	Tomatoes	225g
2oz	Stuffed olives	50g
	Salt	
	Cayenne pepper	

Soak beans in 1 pint (600 ml) water overnight in a large saucepan. The next day, simmer for 1 hour.

Heat oil in flameproof casserole and brown chicken all over. Remove from pan. Peel and chop onions; peel and crush garlic. Cook in casserole till golden. Add chilli powder and cook for 5 minutes. Return chicken with stock and simmer for 55 minutes.

Blanch, peel and chop tomatoes. Slice olives. Drain beans. Add all to casserole. Cook for 10 minutes, then season with salt and cayenne pepper.

Chicken with aubergine

Overall timing 50 minutes

Freezing Not suitable

To serve 4

1	Aubergine	1
	Salt and pepper	
1	Green pepper	1
2	Large onions	2
6 tbsp	Oil	6x15ml
4	Chicken pieces	4
¾ pint	Tomato juice	400ml
12oz	Ripe tomatoes	350g

Slice the aubergine. Sprinkle with salt and leave for 15 minutes. Meanwhile, deseed and slice the pepper. Peel and slice the onions.

Heat the oil in a flameproof casserole, add the chicken and fry over a moderate heat, turning frequently, till browned all over. Remove from the pan and reserve.

Add the onions and pepper and fry for 5 minutes. Return the chicken to the casserole, add the tomato juice and seasoning and bring to the boil.

Rinse the aubergine and pat dry on kitchen paper. Add to the chicken, cover and simmer for 25 minutes.

Blanch, peel and quarter the tomatoes. Add to the chicken and cook for a further 5 minutes. Serve with plain boiled rice and a green salad.

Pot au feu

Overall timing 4 hours

Freezing Not suitable

To serve 6		
1	Onion	1
2	Cloves	2
2	Celery stalks	2
1 tbsp	Chopped parsley	15 ml
4 pints	Water	2.2 litres
	Salt and pepper	
1	Cow heel	1
$\frac{1}{2}$	Boiling chicken	$\frac{1}{2}$
2	Leeks	2
1	Carrot	1
2	Potatoes	2

Peel onion and spike with cloves. Chop celery. Put into a flameproof casserole with the parsley, water and seasoning. Bring to the boil, then add cow heel and chicken. Reduce heat and simmer for 3 hours, skimming occasionally.

Remove cow heel and chicken from pan. Cut meat off bones in small chunks. Trim and thinly slice leeks. Peel and slice carrot. Peel and chop potatoes.

Strain stock and return to pan. Add meat and vegetables. Bring back to the boil, then reduce heat and simmer for 30 minutes. Serve hot with toasted bread.

Rabbit with prunes

Overall timing 2 hours plus marination

Freezing Not suitable

To serve 4–6		
$2\frac{1}{2}$ lb	Ovenready rabbit	1.1 kg
1	Small onion	1
1	Bay leaf	1
$\frac{1}{2}$ pint	Dry white wine	300 ml
3	Carrots	3
8 oz	Belly of pork	225 g
4 oz	Plump prunes	125 g
2 tbsp	Redcurrant jelly	2x15 ml
$\frac{1}{2}$ pint	Hot chicken stock	300 ml
	Salt and pepper	

Cut rabbit into neat pieces. Put into a shallow dish. Peel and slice onion and add to rabbit with bay leaf and wine. Marinate overnight.

Preheat the oven to 325°F (170°C) Gas 3.

Peel and chop carrots. Derind pork and cut into strips. Lift rabbit out of marinade and place in casserole. Stone prunes and fill centres with some of pork strips. Add to casserole with carrots and rest of pork. Strain marinade over rabbit.

Stir redcurrant jelly into stock and add to casserole with seasoning. Cover tightly and bake for about $1\frac{1}{2}$ hours till rabbit is tender.

Garlic chicken

Overall timing $1\frac{3}{4}$ hours

Freezing Not suitable

To serve 4

2 oz	Butter	50 g
1 tbsp	Oil	15 ml
8	Chicken legs and wings	8
	Salt and pepper	
1	Whole garlic bulb	1
$\frac{1}{4}$ pint	Dry white wine	150 ml
$\frac{3}{4}$ pint	Hot milk	400 ml
1 teasp	Cornflour	5 ml
2 tbsp	Single cream	2x15 ml
$\frac{1}{4}$ teasp	Cayenne pepper	1.25 ml

Heat half the butter and the oil in a flameproof casserole. Add the chicken and brown on all sides. Season and cook for 10–15 minutes over a low heat. Remove chicken from pan and keep warm.

Peel and crush all the garlic cloves. Add remaining butter to casserole with garlic and cook over a low heat, stirring with a wooden spoon, till soft.

Add the wine, bring to the boil and simmer for 3 minutes. Replace chicken in casserole and pour in hot milk. Cover and simmer for 20–30 minutes.

Blend the cornflour and cream in a bowl. Stir in 3 tbsp (3x15 ml) of cooking liquor from casserole and add cayenne pepper. Stir cream mixture into casserole and simmer for 2–3 minutes.

Put chicken pieces into a warmed serving dish and spoon sauce over. Serve with green beans and mashed potatoes.

Jugged hare

Overall timing 2½ hours plus marinating

Freezing Not suitable

To serve 10

7½ lb	Ovenready hare with the blood	3.4 kg
2 tbsp	White wine	2x15 ml
4 oz	Calf's liver	125 g
2½ pints	Red wine	1.5 litres
1	Celery stalk	1
3	Onions	3
1	Carrot	1
1	Garlic clove	1
1	Bouquet garni	1
6	Juniper berries	6
4	Black peppercorns	4
3	Cloves	3
1	Small cinnamon stick	1
	Salt and pepper	
	Plain flour	
2 oz	Butter	50 g

Keep blood in a bowl, mixed with white wine to prevent coagulation, until ready to use.

Cut hare into serving pieces. Put in a bowl with liver, heart and sliced calf's liver. Pour over red wine. Trim and chop celery. Peel and chop 2 onions, the carrot and garlic. Add these vegetables to bowl with bouquet garni, juniper berries, peppercorns, spices and seasoning. Let marinate for 24 hours, turning occasionally.

Drain hare, reserving marinade, pat dry and coat with flour. Peel and chop remaining onion. Heat butter in a flameproof casserole and fry onion till soft. Add hare pieces and brown on all sides. Add reserved marinade (except livers), bring to the boil and simmer gently, covered, for 1½ hours.

Add livers and cook for a further 30 minutes. If sauce is too thick, add some hot water.

Remove hare pieces. Strain cooking liquid and return it to casserole. Stir in blood. Return hare pieces and reheat.

Chicken Kiev

Overall timing $1\frac{1}{2}$ hours

Freezing Suitable: egg, crumb and fry after thawing

To serve 4

4 oz	Softened butter	125 g
2 tbsp	Lemon juice	2x15 ml
1	Garlic clove	1
1 tbsp	Chopped parsley	15 ml
	Salt and pepper	
4	Boneless chicken breasts	4
	Oil for frying	
3 tbsp	Plain flour	3x15 ml
1	Egg	1
3 tbsp	Fresh white breadcrumbs	3x15 ml

Work together the butter and lemon juice until smooth. Peel and crush the garlic and add to the butter with the parsley and seasoning. Mix well. Shape into a cylinder, wrap in foil and place in freezer for 1 hour to firm.

Place the chicken breasts between two sheets of dampened greaseproof paper on a flat surface and beat flat with a heavy knife or wooden mallet until thin.

Heat the oil in a deep-fryer to 350°F (170°C).

Place a piece of butter on each chicken breast. Roll chicken round butter and secure with a cocktail stick. Coat each piece of chicken all over with the flour, then dip in the beaten egg to cover and finally in the breadcrumbs, pressing them on well. Fry for 12–15 minutes until golden brown. Drain on kitchen paper, remove cocktail sticks and serve immediately with lemon wedges and a green salad.

Chicken breasts with cheese cream

Overall timing 40 minutes

Freezing Not suitable

To serve 4

4	Boneless chicken breasts	4
	Plain flour	
	Salt and pepper	
3oz	Butter	75g
5 tbsp	Dry white wine	5x15ml
5 tbsp	Chicken stock	5x15ml
4oz	Cream cheese	125g
1 tbsp	Milk	15ml
	Truffles (optional)	

Lightly beat the chicken breasts to flatten, without making any holes. Coat with seasoned flour. Heat 2oz (50g) of the butter in a frying pan and fry chicken breasts until golden on both sides.

Add wine and stock and bring to the boil. Cover and simmer gently for 20 minutes till chicken is tender.

Meanwhile, put cheese, remaining butter, milk and seasoning in a saucepan. Heat gently, stirring, till smooth and creamy.

Preheat the grill.

Transfer chicken breasts to a flameproof serving dish. Spread cheese cream over them and grill till lightly browned. Serve garnished with sliced truffles, if liked.

Dinner-party duck

Overall timing $1\frac{1}{2}$ hours

Freezing Not suitable

To serve 6–8

2x4lb	Ovenready ducks	2x1.8kg
	Salt and pepper	
2oz	Butter	50g
2	Oranges	2
8fl oz	Port	220ml
1lb	Stoned cherries	450g
2 tbsp	Redcurrant jelly	2x15ml
4 tbsp	Cherry brandy	4x15ml

Dry ducks thoroughly. Prick all over with a fork. Season inside of ducks with salt and pepper. Melt butter in a flameproof casserole. When it is very hot, add ducks and brown on all sides for 15–20 minutes turning frequently to avoid sticking.

Wash the oranges and grate finely to obtain 1 tbsp (15ml) zest (the coloured part, not the pith). Add the orange zest, half the port and seasoning to the casserole. Cover and cook for 1 hour, turning the birds over halfway through cooking time.

Remove ducks from casserole and keep warm. Skim any excess fat from the surface of the cooking liquor. Add remaining port. Boil fast to reduce by one third. Add cherries, redcurrant jelly and cherry brandy and mix in well. Cover and cook gently for 5 minutes.

Carve ducks and arrange pieces on serving dish. Strain sauce and arrange cherries over ducks. Pour sauce into gravy boat. Serve with potatoes and chicory salad.

Pastry-wrapped stuffed chicken

Overall timing $2\frac{1}{4}$ hours

Freezing Not suitable

To serve 4

3 lb	Ovenready chicken	1.4 kg
	Salt	
1 oz	Butter	25 g
12 oz	Shortcrust pastry	350 g
1	Egg	1
Stuffing		
8 oz	Mushrooms	225 g
1 oz	Butter	25 g
2 tbsp	Sherry	2x15 ml
	Salt and pepper	
6 oz	Chicken livers	175 g
1	Small onion	1
2 oz	Dried breadcrumbs	50 g

First make stuffing. Slice mushrooms. Melt butter in a pan and fry mushrooms for 3 minutes. Add sherry and cook for 3 minutes. Season with salt and pepper.

Finely chop chicken livers. Peel and finely chop onion. Add both to pan with breadcrumbs and mix well. Heat gently for 5 minutes.

Season chicken inside and out with salt. Stuff with liver mixture and close the opening. Melt butter in a roasting tin and brown chicken on all sides for 20 minutes.

Preheat the oven to 400°F (200°C) Gas 6.

Roll out dough on a lightly floured surface till about $\frac{1}{4}$ inch (6mm) thick and large enough to wrap round chicken. Remove chicken from roasting tin. Drain and allow to cool slightly, then place, breast side down, on dough. Moisten edges and wrap dough round chicken. Press edges together well.

Place chicken on greased baking tray with seam underneath. Use dough trimmings to decorate top. Brush with beaten egg and bake for $1\frac{1}{2}$–$1\frac{3}{4}$ hours. If pastry shows signs of overbrowning, cover with foil.

Duck with orange

Overall timing $1\frac{1}{4}$ hours

Freezing Not suitable

To serve 4

4lb	Ovenready duck	1.8kg
	Salt and pepper	
2oz	Butter	50g
4fl oz	White wine	120ml
3	Oranges	3
1oz	Sugar	25g
1 tbsp	Vinegar	15ml
$\frac{1}{2}$	Lemon	$\frac{1}{2}$
4fl oz	Duck or chicken stock	120ml
2 tbsp	Brandy	2x15ml

Sprinkle duck all over with salt and pepper. Prick with a fork. Heat butter in a flameproof casserole and brown duck on all sides. Cover and cook for about 45 minutes till duck is tender, basting occasionally with wine.

Meanwhile, peel two oranges thinly and cut rind into thin strips. Blanch strips in boiling water for 2–3 minutes, then drain well. Dissolve sugar in vinegar, add strips of rind and boil until mixture caramelizes. Set aside. Squeeze juice from the two oranges and from the lemon.

When duck is ready, place on a warmed serving platter and keep hot. Skim fat from cooking juices, then gradually stir in stock, orange and lemon juices and brandy. Bring to the boil. Add caramelized mixture and stir well. Simmer for 8–10 minutes till reduced.

Pour sauce over duck. Garnish with remaining orange, peeled and segmented.

Roast duck with peaches

Overall timing $1\frac{1}{4}$ hours

Freezing Not suitable

To serve 4

$3\frac{1}{2}$ lb	Ovenready duck	1.6kg
	Salt and pepper	
1oz	Split almonds	25g
2 teasp	Caster sugar	2x5ml
3 tbsp	Vinegar or lemon juice	3x15ml
$\frac{1}{4}$ pint	Peach nectar	150ml
4	Fresh peaches	4
2 tbsp	Amaretto di Saronno liqueur	2x15ml

Preheat the oven to 400°F (200°C) Gas 6.

Wipe duck and sprinkle inside and out with salt and pepper. Prick all over with a fork and place on wire rack in roasting tin. Roast for 50 minutes to 1 hour until tender.

Meanwhile, spread almonds on a baking tray and toast towards the top of the oven for 10 minutes till golden brown. Remove and reserve.

Heat sugar gently in a hot saucepan till it just begins to brown. Stir in the vinegar or lemon juice. Bring to boil and boil fast till reduced by half. Add peach nectar to pan and bring to the boil, stirring, until sauce thickens.

Peel fresh peaches. Cut in half and remove stones. Make "fans" of 2 of the halves by slicing each one through almost to the end. Finely slice other halves. Add slices and fans to the sauce with the Amaretto. Heat through gently for 2 minutes, basting frequently.

Remove duck from roasting tin and place on serving plate. Remove peach fans from sauce and place on top. Spoon sauce over and sprinkle with toasted almonds. Garnish with lemon baskets.

French-style roast goose

Overall timing 3 hours

Freezing Not suitable

To serve 8

2	Large onions	2
3	Celery stalks	3
4oz	Butter	125g
6oz	Fresh breadcrumbs	175g
	Salt and pepper	
1 teasp	Grated nutmeg	5ml
1 tbsp	Chopped fresh sage *or*	15ml
2 teasp	Dried sage	2x5ml
9lb	Ovenready goose	4.1kg
1lb	Cooking apples	450g

Preheat the oven to 400°F (200°C) Gas 6.

Peel and chop onions. Chop celery. Heat 2oz (50g) of the butter in a frying pan and fry onions and celery until golden. Remove from heat and stir in breadcrumbs, salt, pepper, nutmeg and sage.

Wipe goose, stuff with the breadcrumb mixture and close up. Prick all over with a fork. Spread 1oz (25g) butter over the legs and wings and season with salt and pepper. Place goose on rack in roasting tin and cover breast with greased greaseproof or foil. Roast for about 2½ hours or until juices run clear when the leg is pierced with a skewer.

Peel, core and slice apples. Put into a pan with the remaining butter and cook gently till pulpy.

Place goose on warmed serving plate and surround with roast potatoes. Serve apple sauce separately.

Turkey stuffed with chestnuts

Overall timing $2\frac{3}{4}$ hours

Freezing Not suitable

To serve 6–8

$1\frac{1}{4}$ lb	Roasted chestnuts	600 g
8 oz	Tenderised prunes	225 g
2	Large apples	2
4 oz	Butter	125 g
8 oz	Sausagemeat	225 g
$7\frac{1}{2}$ lb	Ovenready turkey	3.4 kg
4–6	Streaky bacon rashers	4–6
	Salt and pepper	
4 tbsp	Dry white wine	4x15 ml
	Turkey giblet stock	

Preheat oven to 350°F (180°C) Gas 4.

Peel chestnuts. Stone and chop prunes (if not tenderised, they will need to be soaked first). Peel, core and chop apples. Heat butter in a frying pan, add chestnuts, prunes, apples and sausagemeat and cook, stirring occasionally, for 10–15 minutes.

Put chestnut mixture into turkey and sew up opening. Truss turkey and cover breast with bacon rashers. Sprinkle with salt and pepper.

Place turkey in a roasting tin and pour over wine. Roast for 2 hours, basting occasionally with wine in tin and stock as needed. Remove bacon about 30 minutes before cooking is finished so breast can brown. Let rest for 10 minutes before carving.

Partridge with grapes

Overall timing 45 minutes

Freezing Not suitable

To serve 4

2–4	Ovenready partridges	2–4
2–4	Slices of pork fat	2–4
	Salt and pepper	
5 tbsp	Dry white wine	5x15 ml
4 oz	Seedless white grapes	125 g
½ oz	Butter	15 g

Preheat oven to 400°F (200°C) Gas 6.

Cover breasts of partridges with pork fat, tying it on with string, and keeping legs parallel with bodies. Sprinkle with salt and pepper. Arrange partridges in a roasting tin and roast for about 30 minutes, basting from time to time with the fat that will collect in the tin.

Remove the partridges from the tin, discard the pork fat and keep the birds hot.

Pour off the fat from the tin, leaving the sediment. Add the wine and stir over a low heat to dissolve the sediment. Add the grapes (peeled, if liked) and heat through. Remove the grapes with a slotted spoon and arrange around the partridges. Swirl the butter into the cooking juices and serve this sauce separately.

Pheasant on croûtons

Overall timing 1–$1\frac{1}{4}$ hours

Freezing Not suitable

To serve 2–3

1	Bay leaf	1
2	Juniper berries	2
4	Slices of prosciutto or streaky bacon	4
2oz	Butter	50g
	Salt and pepper	
2–$2\frac{1}{2}$lb	Ovenready pheasant (preferably a hen)	900g–1.1kg
6 tbsp	Dry white wine	6x15ml
2 tbsp	Chicken stock	2x15ml
2–3	Slices of white bread	2–3
	Oil and butter for frying	

Chop bay leaf, juniper berries and 2 slices of prosciutto or derinded bacon together and mix with 1 tbsp of the butter. Season with salt and pepper. Shape into a ball and place inside pheasant. Truss bird and cover breast with remaining prosciutto or bacon.

Heat remaining butter in a flameproof casserole, add pheasant and brown on all sides. Add wine and stock and bring to the boil. Cover and cook gently for 45–50 minutes or till pheasant is tender, basting occasionally with cooking juices.

Meanwhile, remove crusts from bread and cut each slice into four triangles. Fry in mixed oil and butter till golden brown on both sides. Drain on kitchen paper.

Arrange croûtons on a warmed serving platter. Untruss pheasant and place on croûtons. Pour over cooking juices before serving.

Roast quail in vine leaves

Overall timing 45 minutes

Freezing Not suitable

To serve 4

4	Vine leaves	4
4	Ovenready quails	4
	Salt and pepper	
4	Streaky bacon rashers	4
2oz	Butter	50g
4 tbsp	Oil	4x15ml
4	Thin slices of bread	4

Preheat the oven to 425°F (220°C) Gas 7.

Wash the vine leaves and pat dry with kitchen paper. Wipe and dry the quails and season. Derind and stretch the bacon rashers. Place a vine leaf over the breast of each quail, wrap a rasher of bacon around each and secure with wooden cocktail sticks or fine string.

Heat half the butter and half the oil in frying pan and fry the quails over a moderate heat for 5 minutes, turning frequently. Transfer the contents of the pan to a roasting tin, place in the centre of the oven and roast for about 15 minutes till quails are tender.

Meanwhile, remove the crusts from the bread. Heat rest of butter and oil in the frying pan and fry slices on both sides till golden. Arrange on a warmed serving dish and keep hot.

Remove cocktail sticks or string and the bacon and vine leaves from the quails and arrange on the fried bread. Serve immediately with the crispy bacon, game chips and redcurrant jelly.

Grouse with truffles

Overall timing About 1 hour

Freezing Not suitable

To serve 4

4	Small ovenready grouse	4
	Salt and pepper	
	Truffles	
4	Slices of prosciutto or streaky bacon	4
2oz	Butter	50g
2 tbsp	Brandy	2x15ml
	Chicken or game stock	

Sprinkle grouse with salt and pepper. Put a slice of truffle in each bird. Wrap birds in prosciutto or bacon.

Heat butter in a flameproof casserole, add grouse and brown on all sides. Add brandy, heat and set alight. When flames die down, add enough stock to cover bottom of casserole. Cover and cook for 25–30 minutes till grouse are tender, adding more stock as necessary.

Remove grouse from casserole, discard prosciutto (or serve with birds) and arrange on a warmed serving platter. Add a little chopped truffle to the cooking juices, heat through and spoon over the grouse.

Turkey croquettes

Overall timing 45 minutes

Freezing Suitable: thaw, then reheat in moderately hot oven for about 20 minutes or deep fry for about 5 minutes (do not overbrown)

To serve 4–6

1 lb	Cooked turkey meat	450 g
9 oz	Butter	250 g
1	Small onion	1
4 oz	Plain flour	125 g
½ pint	Milk	300 ml
	Salt and pepper	
2	Egg yolks	2
2 oz	Grated Cheddar cheese	50 g
2 tbsp	Chopped chives	2x15 ml
1	Egg	1
4 oz	Dried breadcrumbs	125 g
2 tbsp	Oil	2x15 ml

Finely chop or mince the turkey. Melt 3 oz (75 g) butter in a saucepan. Peel and finely chop the onion. Add it to the butter and when soft, stir in 3 oz (75 g) flour. Cook for 2 minutes over a low heat, stirring constantly. Add the milk, salt and pepper and stir till thickened. Cook for 5 minutes.

Remove from the heat and beat in the egg yolks, cheese and chives. Turn into a mixing bowl and mix in the turkey well. Leave to cool. (Refrigerate if necessary, stirring from time to time.)

Using your hands shape the mixture into 2 inch (5 cm) round flat patties and lightly coat them with remaining flour. Beat the egg in a shallow dish with a little water. Dip each patty into the egg, coating them completely and then into the breadcrumbs, pressing the crumbs on well with your hands or a spatula. Heat half the remaining butter with the oil and fry the patties until they are golden brown, about 4 minutes each side. Add more butter or oil if necessary.

Turkey or chicken divan

Overall timing 1 hour

Freezing Not suitable

To serve 4

1	Small onion	1
1	Small carrot	1
1	Celery stalk	1
1 pint	Milk	600 ml
1	Bay leaf	1
2 oz	Butter	50 g
2 oz	Plain flour	50 g
	Salt and pepper	
$\frac{1}{2}$ teasp	Grated nutmeg	2.5 ml
4 tbsp	Double cream	4x15 ml
6 oz	Grated cheese	175 g
1 lb	Broccoli	450 g
1 lb	Cooked turkey or chicken meat	450 g

Peel and chop onion and carrot. Trim and chop celery. Place vegetables in a saucepan with milk and bay leaf and bring slowly to the boil. Remove from the heat, cover and infuse for 15 minutes. Strain milk.

Melt butter in a clean saucepan, stir in flour and cook for 1 minute. Gradually stir in milk and bring to the boil, stirring. Simmer till thickened. Remove from the heat and season with salt, pepper and nutmeg. Stir in cream and 4 oz (125 g) of the cheese till smooth.

Preheat oven to 400°F (200°C) Gas 6.

Cook broccoli in boiling salted water for 5 minutes till just tender. Drain well.

Cut turkey or chicken into bite-size pieces. Place in buttered ovenproof dish and arrange broccoli around. Pour cheese sauce over and sprinkle with remaining cheese. Bake for 30 minutes till browned and bubbling.

Turkey noodle bake

Overall timing 1½ hours

Freezing Not suitable

To serve 4

4oz	Button mushrooms	125g
8oz	Noodles	225g
	Salt and pepper	
3 tbsp	Plain flour	3x15ml
1	Chicken stock cube	1
¼ teasp	Paprika	1.25ml
5 tbsp	Single cream	5x15ml
8oz	Cooked turkey meat	225g
2oz	Cheddar cheese	50g
1oz	Fresh breadcrumbs	25g
½oz	Butter	15g

Wipe and slice the mushrooms. Cook the noodles in boiling salted water for about 5 minutes till tender. Drain the noodles thoroughly, reserving 1 pint (600ml) of the cooking water.

Blend the flour in a small bowl with a little of the measured cooking water. Put rest of water in a saucepan, stir in blended flour, crumbled stock cube, salt, pepper and paprika. Bring to the boil, stirring. Reduce the heat and add the mushrooms. Simmer for 10 minutes.

Preheat the oven to 350°F (180°C) Gas 4. Grease an 8 inch (20cm) soufflé dish.

Remove pan from heat and stir in cream.

Spread half the drained noodles over the bottom of the soufflé dish. Dice the turkey and arrange half over the noodles. Cover with half the sauce. Repeat the layers, finishing with sauce. Grate cheese and scatter over top. Sprinkle with breadcrumbs and dot with butter. Bake for 30 minutes.

Turkey salad mould

Overall timing 40 minutes

Freezing Not suitable

To serve 4

1 lb	Cooked turkey meat	450 g
4 oz	Canned sweetcorn kernels	125 g
1	Onion	1
$\frac{1}{2}$	Red pepper	$\frac{1}{2}$
$\frac{1}{2}$	Green pepper	$\frac{1}{2}$
1	Celery stalk	1
$\frac{1}{4}$	Cucumber	$\frac{1}{4}$
1	Small green apple	1
2 oz	Peanuts	50 g
1 oz	Raisins	25 g
	Salt and pepper	
$\frac{1}{4}$ pint	Thick mayonnaise	150 ml
1 tbsp	Curry powder (optional)	15 ml
$\frac{1}{4}$ teasp	Cayenne pepper	1.25 ml
$\frac{1}{2}$ tbsp	Lemon juice	7.5 ml
	Watercress sprigs	

Cut the turkey into cubes. Drain the canned corn well. Peel and chop the onion. Deseed and chop the peppers. Slice the celery finely. Peel and dice the cucumber. Peel and chop the apple. Add the peanuts, raisins, salt and pepper to the above ingredients and mix well together in a large bowl.

In a small bowl mix the mayonnaise, curry powder if used, cayenne and lemon juice. Stir the mayonnaise into the turkey salad and mix well.

Line a large ring mould with cling film (to facilitate unmoulding) and spoon the turkey mixture into it. Press it down firmly. Unmould on to a serving plate, garnish with watercress and serve with rice.

Mexican snacks

Overall timing 30 minutes

Freezing Not suitable

To serve 4

1	Round lettuce	1
8 oz	Cooked turkey meat	225 g
2	Firm tomatoes	2
1	Large onion	1
1	Avocado	1
	Oil for deep frying	
4	Canned tortillas	4
8 oz	Canned refried beans	225 g
¼ pint	Soured cream	150 ml

Wash and dry the lettuce and shred finely. Cut the turkey into thin strips. Wash the tomatoes and cut each into 4 slices. Peel and thinly slice the onion in rings. Halve the avocado, remove the stone and cut flesh into 16 slices, discarding the skin.

Heat the oil in a deep-fryer to 360°F (180°C). Add the tortillas and fry for about 2 minutes till golden brown, keeping them flat by turning them frequently. Remove with a draining spoon and drain on kitchen paper.

Spread heated beans over each tortilla, cover with lettuce and then a layer of turkey. Top with tomato and garnish with onion rings, a spoonful of soured cream and avocado slices. Arrange on lettuce-lined serving dish and serve immediately with a side dish of pickled chillies.

Cantonese rice

Overall timing 50 minutes

Freezing Not suitable

To serve 4

6	Dried Chinese mushrooms	6
2	Small onions	2
8 oz	Streaky bacon	225 g
8 oz	Cooked chicken meat	225 g
3 tbsp	Oil	3x15 ml
1 lb	Cooked rice	450 g
4 oz	Shelled prawns	125 g
1 tbsp	Chopped chives	15 ml
	Salt and pepper	
¼ teasp	Cayenne pepper	1.25 ml
2	Eggs	2

Soak mushrooms in warm water for 30 minutes. Peel onions and cut into thin wedges. Derind and dice bacon; finely shred chicken. Drain and chop mushrooms, discarding stalks.

Heat oil in frying pan and stir-fry onions, mushrooms, bacon and chicken for 3–4 minutes. Add rice and stir-fry for 1 minute. Stir in prawns, chives, salt and cayenne; cook for 3 minutes.

Meanwhile, beat eggs with seasoning and 1 tbsp (15 ml) cold water. Make a thin omelette, roll up and shred finely. Pile rice mixture on warmed serving dish and top with omelette.

Chicken à la king

Overall timing 35 minutes

Freezing Suitable

To serve 4

1 lb	Cooked chicken meat	450 g
1	Onion	1
1	Large green pepper	1
2 oz	Butter	50 g
2 oz	Plain flour	50 g
2 tbsp	Cold milk	2x15 ml
½ pint	Warm milk	300 ml
	Salt and pepper	
	Grated nutmeg	
2 tbsp	Sherry	2x15 ml

Cut chicken into small pieces. Peel and finely chop onion. Deseed pepper and finely chop half of it. Melt the butter in a saucepan and gently fry onion and chopped pepper till onion is transparent.

Stir in the flour with a wooden spoon, then the cold milk. Remove from heat and gradually add the warm milk. Bring to the boil. Season with salt, pepper and a pinch of nutmeg. Reduce heat and simmer gently for 15 minutes.

Add chicken and sherry and cook for 5 minutes more. Stir frequently during this time to prevent mixture sticking.

Meanwhile, slice the remaining pepper and blanch in boiling water for 5 minutes.

Place chicken and sauce on a warmed serving plate and surround with the pepper slices. Serve with boiled rice or noodles.

Welsh chicken pie

Overall timing 1 hour

Freezing Not suitable

To serve 6

1½ lb	Cooked chicken meat	700 g
4 oz	Cooked tongue	125 g
1	Onion	1
4	Leeks	4
3	Celery stalks	3
2 oz	Butter	50 g
1 teasp	Ground mace	5 ml
1 tbsp	Chopped parsley	15 ml
½ pint	Chicken stock	300 ml
	Salt and pepper	
12 oz	Shortcrust pastry	350 g
1	Egg	1

Preheat oven to 400°F (200°C) Gas 6.

Chop chicken into medium-size pieces. Cut the tongue into strips. Peel and thinly slice onion. Trim leeks, then cut into thin slices. Trim and finely chop the celery. Melt butter.

Put chicken, tongue and prepared vegetables in a bowl with mace, parsley and butter and mix well. Place in a large pie dish and add stock and seasoning.

Roll out dough and place on dish. Press edge to dish to seal. Lightly beat the egg and brush over the dough. Bake for 40 minutes, or until the pastry is golden. Serve immediately with mashed potatoes.

Chicken fritters

Overall timing 40 minutes

Freezing Not suitable

To serve 4

$2\frac{1}{2}$ lb	Cooked chicken meat (in large pieces)	1.1 kg
	Salt	
2 tbsp	Chopped chives or parsley	2x15 ml
2 tbsp	Lemon juice	2x15 ml
1 tbsp	Olive oil	15 ml
	Oil for frying	
	Plain flour	
Batter		
4 tbsp	Plain flour	4x15 ml
$\frac{1}{4}$ pint	Water	150 ml
1	Large egg	1

Put chicken in a deep dish and season with salt, chives or parsley, lemon juice and olive oil. Leave to marinate for at least 30 minutes, turning occasionally.

Meanwhile, make the batter. Mix the flour well with a pinch of salt and the water. Separate egg. Add yolk to flour mixture and beat till smooth. Just before frying, whisk egg white to a stiff foam and fold into batter.

Heat about $\frac{1}{2}$ inch (1 cm) oil in a frying pan. Coat chicken pieces with flour, then dip in batter. Fry in oil for about 3 minutes till golden. Drain on kitchen paper and serve hot.

Macaroni bake

Overall timing $1\frac{3}{4}$ hours

Freezing Not suitable

To serve 6

4 oz	Chicken livers	125 g
2 oz	Butter	50 g
8 oz	Cooked chicken meat	225 g
2 oz	Smoked ham	50 g
$\frac{1}{4}$ pint	White sauce	150 ml
1	Egg	1
	Salt and pepper	
1 lb	Ripe tomatoes	450 g
1	Onion	1
2	Garlic cloves	2
1 teasp	Sugar	5 ml
1 tbsp	Chopped fresh basil	15 ml
12 oz	Long macaroni	350 g
2 oz	Grated Parmesan cheese	50 g

Wash and chop livers. Heat 1 oz (25 g) butter in a frying pan and fry livers for 5 minutes, turning frequently. Chop chicken and ham. Place in a blender or food processor and add livers and their cooking juices, sauce, egg and seasoning. Process till smooth. Chill.

Blanch, peel and chop tomatoes. Peel and chop onion. Heat remaining butter in a saucepan and fry onion with peeled and crushed garlic for 5 minutes. Add tomatoes, sugar, basil and seasoning and bring to the boil. Cover and simmer gently for 15 minutes.

Meanwhile, break macaroni into 4 inch (10 cm) lengths and cook in boiling salted water for 5 minutes. Drain. Fill with liver stuffing, using a piping bag.

Preheat oven to 350°F (180°C) Gas 4. Process tomato sauce in blender or food processor. Spread one-third over bottom of ovenproof dish, then layer macaroni and remaining sauce on top.

Sprinkle Parmesan over and bake for 20 minutes till golden. Garnish with basil leaves and serve.

Hot ham and chicken pie

Overall timing $2\frac{1}{2}$ hours

Freezing Not suitable

To serve 4

1 oz	Butter	25 g
6 oz	Plain flour	175 g
1 pint	Hot chicken stock	600 ml
3 tbsp	Single cream	3x15 ml
	Salt and pepper	
	Grated nutmeg	
7 fl oz	Water	200 ml
2 oz	Lard	50 g
4 oz	Cooked ham	125 g
4 oz	Button mushrooms	125 g
1 tbsp	Chopped parsley	15 ml
$1\frac{3}{4}$ lb	Cooked chicken meat (cut into pieces)	750 g
4	Hard-boiled egg yolks	4
1	Egg	1

Melt butter in a saucepan and stir in 2 oz (50 g) of the flour. Gradually stir in the stock until well blended and thickened. Add cream, salt, pepper and a pinch of nutmeg. Stir well, then set aside.

In a saucepan, bring the water to the boil, cut lard into pieces, add to pan and leave to boil for 10 minutes. Pour into a bowl, add remaining flour and mix to a soft dough. Cover with a cloth and leave in a warm place for 10 minutes.

Preheat oven to 325°F (170°C) Gas 3.

Cut the ham into thin strips. Wipe and slice the mushrooms. Put half the ham, half the mushrooms and the parsley in a buttered ovenproof dish. Cover with half the reserved sauce and arrange chicken pieces on top. Add hard-boiled egg yolks, then top with remaining ham, mushrooms and sauce.

Dampen the edge of the dish. Roll out dough and cover dish with the pastry. Brush with beaten egg and bake for $1\frac{1}{2}$ hours. After 1 hour, cover with foil to prevent over-browning.

Stuffed courgettes

Overall timing $1\frac{1}{2}$ hours

Freezing Suitable: bake from frozen, covered, in 350°F (180°C) Gas 4 oven for about 45 minutes or till hot

To serve 4

5 oz	Mixed cooked chicken and ham	150 g
2 tbsp	Chopped parsley	2x15 ml
1	Garlic clove	1
4 tbsp	Fresh breadcrumbs	4x15 ml
2 tbsp	Grated cheese	2x15 ml
1	Egg	1
4	Large courgettes	4
14 oz	Can of tomatoes	397 g
1 tbsp	Oil	15 ml
2 teasp	Dried basil	2x5 ml

Finely chop chicken and ham. In a bowl, mix together the meat, parsley, peeled and crushed garlic, 2 tbsp (2x15 ml) breadcrumbs, cheese and egg.

Wash courgettes and trim ends. Halve them lengthways. Scoop out centres with a melon baller or small spoon, chop finely and add to bowl. Fill courgette shells with prepared mixture.

Purée drained tomatoes in a blender or push through a sieve. Heat oil in a flameproof casserole, add tomato purée and basil and cook for about 10 minutes. Meanwhile heat the oven to 350°F (180°C) Gas 4.

Add stuffed courgettes to casserole, sprinkle with remaining breadcrumbs, baste with tomato sauce, cover and cook in the oven for 50 minutes. Remove lid for last 10 minutes of cooking to help crisp the topping. Serve hot.

Creamy chicken pancakes

Overall timing $1\frac{1}{4}$ hours

Freezing Suitable

To serve 4

1	Small carrot	1
1	Small onion	1
4oz	Button mushrooms	125g
4	Streaky bacon rashers	4
3oz	Butter	75g
2oz	Plain flour	50g
1 pint	Milk	600ml
	Salt and pepper	
1lb	Cooked chicken meat	450g
4oz	Frozen peas	125g
12	Pancakes (page 28)	12
	Chopped parsley	

Peel and finely chop carrot and onion. Halve mushrooms. Derind and dice bacon. Heat butter in a saucepan, add vegetables and bacon and cook for 2 minutes.

Sprinkle over flour and stir in well. Cook for 1 minute, then gradually stir in milk. Bring to the boil, stirring, and simmer till thickened. Season. Simmer gently for 15 minutes.

Cut chicken into small cubes. Set aside one-quarter of sauce for topping; add chicken and peas to remaining sauce and mix well. Simmer for a further 5 minutes.

Preheat oven to 350°F (180°C) Gas 4.

Divide chicken mixture among pancakes and roll them up. Arrange in a buttered ovenproof dish. Pour remaining sauce over. Dot with remaining butter.

Bake for 15 minutes. Sprinkle with parsley before serving.

Chicken and tongue mould

Overall timing 30 minutes plus chilling

Freezing Not suitable

To serve 6–8

1 pint	Prepared jellied stock	600ml
3 fl oz	Marsala or sherry	90ml
1 tbsp	White wine vinegar	15ml
1 lb	Cooked chicken meat	450g
8 oz	Cooked tongue	225g
	Sprigs of parsley	
Sauce		
4 fl oz	Thick mayonnaise	120ml
1 tbsp	Chopped parsley	15ml
1 tbsp	Anchovy paste	15ml
1 tbsp	French mustard	15ml
1 tbsp	Chopped capers	15ml

Divide the stock in half. To one half add the Marsala or sherry, and to the other add the vinegar. Put some of the vinegar stock into a chilled round mould and tilt to coat the sides and bottom. Chill until nearly set.

Cut the chicken and tongue into strips. Place in the mould and pour in the remaining vinegar stock. Chill until almost set, then pour in the Marsala stock. Chill until completely set.

Mix together the sauce ingredients. Cover and chill.

To serve, dip the mould into hot water, then turn out on to a serving dish. Garnish with parsley sprigs and serve with the sauce.

Chicken pineapple salad

Overall timing 30 minutes plus chilling

Freezing Not suitable

To serve 4–6

4oz	Long grain rice	125g
	Salt and pepper	
4oz	Frozen sweetcorn kernels	125g
1	Celery heart	1
1–$1\frac{1}{2}$lb	Cooked chicken meat	450–700g
8oz	Can of pineapple rings	227g
4	Small firm tomatoes	4
2oz	Black olives	50g
3 tbsp	Salad oil	3x15ml
1 tbsp	Lemon juice	15ml
1 tbsp	Chopped chives	15ml
1	Round lettuce	1
1	Hard-boiled egg	1

Cook the rice in boiling salted water till tender, adding the sweetcorn for the last 5 minutes of cooking. Drain and rinse under cold water, then drain thoroughly.

Trim celery heart and cut into 2 inch (5cm) lengths. Put into a large bowl with the celery leaves. Cut the chicken into bite-size pieces, discarding any skin and bones. Add to the bowl.

Drain the pineapple; chop three of the rings. Quarter the tomatoes and add to the bowl with the chopped pineapple, olives, rice and sweetcorn.

Mix together the oil, lemon juice, chives and seasoning. Pour over the salad and toss lightly. Chill for 30 minutes.

Wash and dry the lettuce and use to line a salad bowl. Pile the salad into the centre and garnish with the remaining pineapple rings and the hard-boiled egg quartered lengthways. Serve with crusty bread.

Double decker sandwich

Overall timing 15 minutes

Freezing Not suitable

To serve 1

1	Small French loaf	1
	Softened butter	
	Lettuce leaves	
1–2	Slices of cooked ham	1–2
	Mayonnaise	
1–2	Slices of Gruyère or Cheddar cheese	1–2
1	Tomato	1
2–3	Slices of cooked chicken	2–3

Trim the ends and the crust from the loaf, then cut it into 3 horizontally. Toast the slices on both sides. Butter 1 slice of toast and cover with lettuce leaves. Arrange the ham on top and dot with mayonnaise. Place the cheese on top.

Butter a second slice of toast on both sides and place on the cheese. Cover with more lettuce, tomato slices and chicken and dot with more mayonnaise. Butter the last slice of toast and place on top of the sandwich, buttered side down.

Index